Patricia L. Mathson, Preschool Coordinator at St. Vincent de Paul Catholic Church in Arlington, Texas, has more than eight years' experience in the field of religious education. Her articles have appeared in major religious education magazines.

This series offers the concerned reader basic guidelines and *practical* applications of religion for today's world. Although decidedly Christian in focus and emphasis, the series embraces all denominations and modes of Bible-based belief relevant to our lives today. All volumes in the Steeple series are originals, freshly written to provide a fresh perspective on current—and yet timeless—human dilemmas. This is a series for our times. Among the books:

How to Read the Bible
James Fischer

How to Live Your Faith
L. Perry Wilbur

A Spiritual Handbook for Women
Dandi Daley Knorr

Temptation: How Christians Can Deal with It
Frances Carroll

With God on Your Side: A Guide to Finding Self-Worth Through Total Faith
Doug Manning

A Daily Key for Today's Christians: 365 Key Texts of the New Testament
William E. Bowles

Walking in the Garden: Inner Peace from the Flowers of God
Paula Connor

How to Bring Up Children in the Catholic Faith
Carol and David Powell

Sex in the Bible: An Introduction to What the Scriptures Teach Us About Sexuality
Michael R. Cosby

How to Talk with God Every Day of the Year: A Book of Devotions for Twelve Positive Months
Frances Hunter

God's Conditions for Prosperity: How to Earn the Rewards of Christian Living
Charles Hunter

Pilgrimages: A Guide to the Holy Places of Europe for Today's Traveler
Paul Lambourne Higgins

Journey into the Light: Lessons of Pain and Joy to Renew Your Energy and Strengthen Your Faith
Dorris Blough Murdock

CREATIVE LEARNING ACTIVITIES FOR RELIGIOUS EDUCATION

A Catalog of Teaching Ideas for Church, School, and Home

PATRICIA L. MATHSON

Illustrated by
Lana Connelly

A SPECTRUM BOOK

Prentice-Hall, Inc., Englewood Cliffs, N.J. 07632

Library of Congress Cataloging in Publication Data

MATHSON, PATRICIA L.
Creative learning activities for religious education.

(Steeple books)
A Spectrum Book.
Bibliography: p.
Includes index.
1. Christian education—Teaching methods. I. Title.
II. Series.
BV1534.M36 1984   268′.432   84-8422
ISBN 0-13-189846-9
ISBN 0-13-189838-8 (pbk.)

This book is available at a special discount when ordered
in bulk quantities. Contact Prentice-Hall, Inc., General
Publishing Division, Special Sales, Englewood Cliffs, N.J. 07632.

Cover design by Hal Siegel
Manufacturing buyer: Doreen Cavallo

A SPECTRUM BOOK

10   9   8   7   6   5   4   3   2   1

ISBN 0-13-189846-9

ISBN 0-13-189838-8   {PBK.}

Printed in the United States of America

Excerpts from THE JERUSALEM BIBLE, copyright © 1966
by Darton, Longman & Todd, Ltd. and Doubleday & Company, Inc.
Used by permission of the publisher.

Prentice-Hall International, Inc., *London*
Prentice-Hall of Australia Pty. Limited, *Sydney*
Prentice-Hall of Canada Inc., *Toronto*
Prentice-Hall of India Private Limited, *New Delhi*
Prentice-Hall of Japan, Inc., *Tokyo*
Prentice-Hall of Southeast Asia Pte. Ltd., *Singapore*
Whitehall Books Limited, *Wellington, New Zealand*
Editora Prentice-Hall do Brasil Ltda., *Rio de Janeiro*

This book is dedicated to my husband, Dick, and my children, Cathy and Steve, who taught me about love.

Contents

Contents

Preface

The focus of this book is on learning activities that help children discover God's presence in their lives through the world and the people around them. Emphasis is on ideas that directly involve the children in the learning process. The activities presented enable the children to learn through experiences in their own lives. Ideas are given for helping children to learn about God's creation, caring for others as Jesus taught, exploring Bible stories, praising God through prayer, and celebrating holidays. Many other topics also are covered.

Different types of activities are explained and practical examples are given of each. A wide range of activities is suggested that will appeal to many different types of students.

This book was written for both beginning and experienced teachers, those who teach in Sunday programs and throughout the week, summer Bible school teachers, program directors and coordinators, pastors, and parents. It is directed to those who work with children from three to eight years of age. Many of the activities can easily be adapted for other ages.

The ideas and activities presented in this book are offered for all those who have the joyful privilege of helping children learn about God and His love for us.

chapter 1

Learning About God

Now is an exciting time to be involved in the field of religious education. Findings in psychology and education have greatly expanded our understanding of how people learn. These principles are being applied in the religious education classroom to help people become knowledgeable and committed Christians.

The emphasis has shifted from what is taught to what is learned. It is the learning that takes place that is important to faith development. No matter what we try to teach children, it is what they learn from us that they will carry with them. In his book *First Things,* Rod Brownfield explains the role of the teacher in religious education: "The right focus, then, is on the student and learning, not on the teacher and teaching. The teacher is properly a facilitator, an enabler, a motivator, a resource person, a creator of an environment in which students can learn for themselves."[1]

Christianity is not facts to be learned, but a way of life. Thus, it is important that individual learning be stressed in religious education. Teachers must stress a personal response to the ideas presented to the children. Faith development is such an individual matter that children must discover the meaning of the lesson for themselves. Only then can they make what they learn a part of their lives.

Learning is a profound event that leads to a change in a person. True learning means not only grasping information, but knowing how to use it in our own lives. Learning is a growth experience that alters a person's way of life.

---

[1]Rod Brownfield, *First Things: A Handbook for Beginners in Religious Education* (Dayton, Oh.: Pflaum Press, 1973), p. 31. Used by permission of Pflaum Press.

In her book *How To Be A Very, Very, Very, Very Good Catechist,* Margaret Timmerman defines learning: "Learning is an experience that affects a change in a person. This might be a change in outlook, in opinion, in understanding, in attitude or in behavior patterns. A desirable kind of learning leads to the right kind of change—one that contributes to the growth of an individual."[2]

Only God can give faith. We cannot impose our beliefs ready-made onto others. We must guide children to discover the meaning of faith in their own lives.

As teachers, we are mediators between God and man. It is our responsibility to pass on God's message of love to the next generation. We must help the children to live the values that Jesus taught. We must help them see that Christianity is a way of living that should have a profound influence on everything they do. As Christians, children will be called upon also to pass on the good news to others.

In order to enable children to learn about God, we must begin with simple concepts appropriate to the age level and development of the children. These ideas can be added to and expanded upon as the children grow and develop. These basic concepts then become the foundation for future learning. Each idea and each experience can help children to expand their faith and love of God.

In order to most effectively help children learn, it is essential that teachers choose specific goals. Goals for younger children should be very simple. Goals for older children can be built upon earlier knowledge and expanded upon in light of their increasing ability to grasp abstract concepts.

A goal should be expressed in one or two sentences. Teachers often try to teach too much and too many different ideas in one class period. The children may end up remembering little. Seldom can more than one concept or idea be covered adequately in an hour of class time.

Each goal should state specifically what it is that the children will be able to do as a result of that lesson. Learning activities should be chosen with the specific goal in mind. In *Teacher Improvement: Practice, Study,* Locke E. Bowman, Jr. gives a list of terms that can be used in goal setting.[3] The following words can be used to describe ways in

---

[2]Margaret Timmerman, M.H.S.H., *How To Be A Very, Very, Very, Very Good Catechist* (Mystic, Conn.: Twenty-Third Publications, 1981), p. 7. Used by permission of Twenty-Third Publications.

[3]Locke E. Bowman, Jr., *Teacher Improvement: Practice, Study* (Scottsdale, Ariz.: The Arizona Experiment, 1976), Form 5. Used by permission of the National Teacher Education Program.

which the children can demonstrate the knowledge gained in a particular lesson:

Tell	Explain
Identify	Recite
Name	Define
Compare	Make
Contrast	Demonstrate
List	Locate
Write	Select
Act out	Draw

Once the goal is set, the methods used to carry it out must be within the realm of the children's understanding. All ideas and concepts presented to the children must be expressed in terms of their own lives and experiences. This is how all people learn. New learning must be related to what people already know. This is especially important with children since religion has so many abstract concepts.

Jesus taught His followers using examples from their own lives. He told parables about shepherds and vineyards and other things familiar to the people to whom He was speaking. We must follow His lead.

All abstract ideas must be tied to concrete examples from the children's lives if learning is to take place. As teachers we must guide the children into making the connection between their lives and God. We can help the children learn about God's presence in their lives through the world and the people around them.

Children are curious and eager to learn. They are constantly learning through everything that they do. Each day is a new opportunity for children to explore their world. Each day they learn more about themselves and their relationships with others.

Religious growth does not take place separately from the growth of an individual. It is part of growing and being a person. Children can learn about God through everything they do. Religious development must be a part of a person's total development as an individual.

The learning activities selected for each lesson must carry out and reinforce the goal and purpose of the lesson. An activity that does not relate to the particular theme of the lesson can interrupt learning. If an activity does not reinforce the lesson, it should not be included in the lesson plan.

A variety of activities helps explain the lesson in different ways so that children will comprehend the material more fully and remember it longer. This multifaceted approach encourages learning in children because their attention spans are limited. Teachers should explain to the children how each activity relates to the subject being studied. The relationship might be obvious to teachers, but not to the students.

Different activities are meaningful for different children. Children have different personalities, different ways of learning, different interests, and different faith backgrounds. One type of activity cannot reach all children. By using a variety of activities in the classroom we can help many different types of children learn about God.

Educational research has shown that children learn by doing. In her book *Create! The Art of Teaching Religion,* Rita Foley states that people remember 20% of what they hear, 30% of what they see, 70% of what they say, and 90% of what they do.[4] Children learn best by being actively involved in the lesson.

Many different types of activities can be used successfully in the classroom with children. Some learning activities that work especially well with children include the following:

Art activities	Pantomime
Singing	Discussion
Role play	Crafts
Celebrations	Shared experiences
Banners	Filmstrips
Games	Speakers
Pictures	Service Projects
Stories	Tapes
Research projects	Displays
Flash cards	Match up cards
Field trips	Puppets

A variety of activities should be used. Activities selected should be suitable to the type of material being presented. The type of activities used should be varied from class to class. A good learning activity used over and over again quickly becomes less effective.

Activities must be geared to the age level and abilities of the children in the class. Difficult activities can frustrate young children. Simple activities that are not in keeping with the developing abilities of older children will not challenge them.

[4]Rita Foley, *Create! The Art of Teaching Religion* (New York: William H. Sadlier, Inc., 1982), p. 39. Used by permission of William H. Sadlier, Inc.

Preparing and developing suitable learning activities takes time. It is essential that teachers carefully prepare each lesson. Children need teachers who are willing to provide the type of classroom environment where learning can take place. Children need teachers who will encourage them to learn and grow in the love of God and neighbor. The children need the guidance of caring teachers if they are to discover the presence of God in their lives.

Hopefully, a successful classroom experience will give the children the desire to continue to seek God throughout their lives. Religious education does not stop with a certain age. It is an ongoing process. We need to encourage children to continue looking for answers.

Our concept of God changes and grows throughout our lives. We must always continue to seek Him in our daily lives. We must help our students learn the necessary skills to continue this search. We must actively involve children in the learning process through various learning activities. In this way they will learn how to seek God. They will be able to make learning about God a part of their lives. We must foster the type of faith development that enables and encourages children to continue to seek God in all that they do.

chapter 2

Fostering a Sense of Self-Esteem

The children's sense of self-esteem affects every facet of their lives. It influences not only how they see themselves, but how they see others. Their self-concept affects their relationships with other people and with God.

The sense of self-concept is one of the most important keys to children's behavior. It affects the way they think, the way they act, how they feel, what they want from life, and their values. Thus, fostering a positive self-concept in children becomes essential in religious education.

If children do not first love themselves, they will not feel worthy of love. They will thus be unable to discover God's love for them. We must help children learn that they are special, wonderful people just as God created them. We must help them know that God loves each of them very much. Children need to feel good about themselves. They need to find joy in being the individuals that they are.

Children must feel secure in themselves before they have enough confidence to reach out with love and trust to others and to God. Jesus said, ". . . You must love your neighbor as yourself" (Matthew 22:39). This presupposes that we love ourselves first. If children do not first learn to love themselves, they will be unable to love God and others. When they learn that they are wonderful, unique people created in God's image, they will have taken the first step toward becoming caring, Christian people.

In his book *TET: Teacher Effectiveness Training*, Dr. Thomas Gordon stresses the importance of helping a child feel accepted: "It is one of those simple paradoxes of life: When a person feels that he is truly accepted by another, as he is, then he is freed to move from there and to begin to think about how he wants to change, how he wants to grow, how he can become different, and how he might become more of what he is capable of being." [1]

Children need to be respected for the individuals that they are. They need freedom to explore being themselves. Children who have little respect for themselves usually have little respect for others. If we are not mindful of the individual needs of children, they will not be able to learn to care about others' needs. Children need to be loved for who they are, not who we would have them be.

We must realize that children have been shaped by people and events in their lives. Children come with different personalities, different interests, and different ways of learning. We must value the children for the people that they are. In this realization we follow Jesus who loved everyone.

Ways in which we can help children develop a sense of self-esteem follow.

Welcoming the Children

Teachers should always be in the classroom to welcome the children as they arrive. What a disappointment it is to a child to hurry eagerly to class to find only an empty classroom. The lesson should be prepared ahead of time and the supplies already assembled so that full attention can be given to the children. This lets them know that we look forward to being with them and that we are happy to see them.

Greet the children by name as they arrive. Try to say something personal to each child such as "We missed you last week" or "I see you brought your bright smile with you." Children like to hear their names used and they like to hear what is special about them.

Children will need to wear nametags the first few weeks. Bright shapes such as a heart, a leaf, or a sun can be cut out of posterboard for nametags. Yarn can be attached to go around the children's necks. This way even young children can put on their nametags without assistance. Teachers also should wear nametags so that the children and their parents can learn the names.

It is also important to be available to the children after class. It shows the children that we care enough about them to wait until the last

---

[1] Reprinted with permission from the book *TET: Teacher Effectiveness Training,* copyright 1974, page 56. Published by David McKay Co., Inc.

child has left. This also gives a child the opportunity to talk to the teacher after everyone else has gone. A child might then feel free to share a problem or just talk with the teacher.

Teachers teach a great deal by example. We teach by what we do as well as by what we say. Our caring actions toward the children send them the message that they are important. In this way we help them experience the love of God through us.

Celebrating Birthdays

Celebrating birthdays in the classroom is a good way to help children feel special. Birthdays are important events to children.

At each class meeting the upcoming birthdays can be celebrated. Those children with summer birthdays can celebrate on the last class day together.

Younger children like to wear special birthday crowns. It makes them feel important. Crowns can be made out of construction paper or from the scalloped bulletin board edging available at teacher supply stores. More than one crown can be on hand in case there is more than one birthday to celebrate on a given class day.

Older children feel proud to wear birthday badges. These can be made by the teacher with the child's name or purchased with self-adhesive backing for the child to wear.

If possible, the teacher or program director can mail a birthday card to each birthday child. Children like to receive mail. Or all the children can sign a handmade card for the birthday child to take home. All the children in the class should join in singing "Happy Birthday" each time there is a birthday.

A bulletin board display can be made featuring each child's name and birthday written inside individual cutouts of birthday cakes. The birthday children can take their paper cakes home as their birthdays occur. The remaining children will see that they also will get a turn to be the center of attention. This also ensures that the teacher will not forget to celebrate each child's important day.

I Am Special Badges

A great esteem-builder for younger children is the "I Am Special Badge." We need to stress to the children how special they are and how God loves each of them. As a visible sign that they are special make each child in the class a badge to wear.

I   AM

SPECIAL

Figure 2-1. I Am Special Badge.

Badges can be cut out of blue construction paper to represent a blue ribbon. Print the words "I am special" on each one (see illustration). Present each child with a badge to wear. Double-stick tape will allow the badges to stick to the children's clothing. They will be proud to wear these badges home.

People Recipes

This activity asks the children to make up recipes that tell about themselves. For this activity the children need to be old enough to know measuring terms such as a cup, a tablespoon, and a dash. Explain to the children that just as many ingredients make up a recipe, so many personal characteristics make a child unique.

The children should print their recipes on individual sheets of paper. An example of a people recipe is:

Recipe for Cathy
1 cup curiosity
3 tbsp. happiness
2 teas. energy
Dash of politeness
A few smiles
Mix the curiosity and happiness. Add energy, politeness, and smiles. Bake well in the love of family and friends.

These recipes help the children to recognize characteristics that make them special. This activity helps the children enjoy being themselves, which is so important. This idea is from the book *Self-Esteem: A Classroom Affair* by Michele and Craig Borba.[2]

Helpers

Each time the class meets, one of the children should be appointed the helper for the day. The helper's duties can include passing out lessons and art supplies. The helper can also assist with clean-up. Having responsibility makes the children feel important. Being a helper gives children a sense of self-worth. They feel good about being useful.

The children can take turns being the teacher's helper. Keep track of their names on the attendance chart so that each child gets an equal number of turns. The children can be appointed at random or the birthday child can be the helper that day. This activity really makes the individual child feel honored and important.

Me Puppets

Puppets are very popular with children and can help children to express their thoughts, ideas, and feelings. Puppets can be especially good for shy children. Sometimes children will feel more free to talk through a puppet than they otherwise would. Children can relate to puppets. They enjoy working with puppets and watching puppets.

Puppets are a terrific way to enable the children to feel that they are special. Children can also use puppets to learn to get along with others. Puppets make learning fun.

[2]From *Self-Esteem: A Classroom Affair* by Michele and Craig Borba, Copyright © 1978 Michele and Craig Borba, p. 29. Published by Winston Press, Inc., 430 Oak Grove, Minneapolis, MN 55403. All rights reserved. Used with permission.

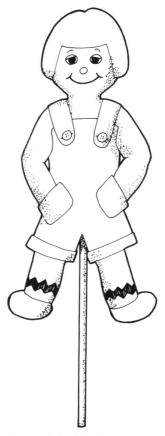

Figure 2-2. Me Puppet.

Children like to make puppets that look like themselves. The shape of a person can be precut for each child out of heavy paper or posterboard. Then the children can fill in features and clothing to look just like themselves. They can draw hair and eyes that are the same color as their own. Young children like to look in mirrors to check eye color and other characteristics. Each puppet can then be taped with masking tape to a wooden dowel, which is used as a handle to make the puppet move (see illustration).

Another way to make a simple puppet is with a small paper plate and a popsickle stick. The children can draw faces that look like theirs on their paper plates. Hair can be colored on the rim of the plate. The puppets can look happy or sad, depending upon how the children want to draw them. A popsickle stick can be taped to the back of each plate to make a convenient handle for the puppet.

Small puppets can be made with construction paper and straws. A simple person shape can be cut out of construction paper for each child. Then the children fill in the puppets to look like themselves. The people shapes are taped to straws. The straws are used as handles to make the puppets talk, sing, or dance.

When the children have finished making their "Me Puppets," they can gather in a circle on the floor. The children can then take turns going around the circle having their puppets tell why they are happy to be who they are.

This activity helps the children to think of things that they like about themselves. They can think of those things that make them special. This activity can lead to positive self-concepts and feelings of self-worth as the children recognize that they are special people. "Me Puppets" help children to see that they are terrific, just as God created them.

Sharing

Children like to feel that they can contribute to the class. Children like to be a part of things. Being able to share builds self-esteem. The students can be asked to bring appropriate items from home to illustrate certain lessons.

If younger children are studying about how God made the animals, they can be asked to bring their favorite stuffed animals to class and tell about them. If older children are studying families, they can bring in pictures of their families. They can tell about family members. This can lead to a discussion of how all families are different, but all are special. Then the pictures can be displayed on the bulletin board.

Notes should go home with the children for these projects so that their parents will know that the children should bring something to class. Parents of absent children should be phoned at home so that those children will know also. It can be very upsetting to children who have been absent to walk into a class where everyone else brought something.

Unfinished Sentences

This activity helps children accept themselves and their feelings. Children need to discover that we all have feelings. They are part of being human. This is something that we can help them discover through listening to other children.

Provide index cards on which are written unfinished sentences for the children to complete. Sentence stubs such as the following can be used:

I feel happy when . . .
I get so angry when . . .
I like people who . . .
I'm lonely when . . .
I'm afraid to . . .
I feel sad when . . .
I wish people would . . .
I feel brave when . . .
I worry about . . .

Teachers and children should sit in a circle. The children take turns picking a card. They may respond to that card if they want to by completing the sentence. There is no right answer. The answer may be funny or serious. Other children should be given the opportunity to respond to the card whether or not the original child does so.

When children see for themselves that others have feelings too, they feel better about themselves. Even the child who does not participate learns by hearing other children voice their feelings. This idea is adapted from the book *100 Ways to Enhance Self-Concept in the Classroom* by Jack Canfield and Harold C. Wells.[3]

Special Student

Every child likes to feel special. A way to help the children in the class feel important is to have a special student display on the bulletin board. One student can be featured each week.

Post a picture of the student. Have the children bring pictures of themselves from home or take their pictures with an instant camera. Print a sign for over the picture that says "This week's special student is" and the child's first and last name. Make other signs to post around the picture with interests of the student. Let that child help decide which information will be put up such as favorite color, sport, and hobbies.

Changing the display each week will give every student an opportunity to be featured during the year. It really builds a positive self-concept for the children to see themselves so honored.

[3]Jack Canfield and Harold C. Wells, *100 Ways to Enhance Self-Concept in the Classroom* (Englewood Cliffs, N.J.: Prentice-Hall, Inc., 1976), p. 65. Adapted by permission.

Award Certificates

Everyone likes to receive an award. Awards are seen as proof of one's worth. Award certificates can be made for the children on half sheets of paper. The giving of awards can be spread throughout the year to make the children feel special. Awards can be for:

Best listener
Most enthusiastic
Good friend
Best smile
Good attendance
Good helper

Be sure each child receives an award. Awards encourage positive behavior. They let children know that their efforts are appreciated.

Me Books

Older children will appreciate the opportunity to become authors of books about very important people—themselves. Two pieces of construction paper can become the cover. Pieces of typing paper can be used for the inside pages. Brads can hold the book together. On the front cover the children can print "A book about" and their name. Then the children can decorate the cover.

The inside pages can be used for all kinds of information about the child. Each page should be titled and the child can draw a picture with crayons to illustrate it. Pages can include the following:

This is me.
Here is my family.
This is what I like to do best of all.
Here is my favorite place to visit.
These are my friends.
Here is where I live.
This is something that I do well.
Here is how I help people.
These are my favorite foods.
This is my favorite game.

The children will be proud to take these books home about themselves. One page could be done each time the class meets. These books can be a source of pride to the children in their interests, their abilities, and themselves.

Thumbprint Pictures

Children like to make thumbprint pictures. Most children are amazed to learn that there are not two people with thumbprints alike in the whole world. Just as God created each individual snowflake different, so each fingerprint and thumbprint are unique. Each child is special.

To make thumbprint pictures, the children press their thumbs first onto a stamp pad and then firmly onto a piece of white paper. Red or blue stamp pads make attractive pictures. Fingerprints can also be used to make pictures, but thumbprints provide a bigger surface with which to work.

After the thumbprints are dry, the children can make pictures out of them. Encourage them to use their imaginations. Thumbprints can be made into almost anything—people, flowers, animals, butterflies, mice, or birds. Colorful, thin marking pens can be used for details.

A butterfly can be made with one thumbprint in the middle for the body. Draw wings on both sides. Then add antennae and eyes to complete the drawing.

A garden of flowers can be made with several thumbprints. Each thumbprint becomes the middle of a flower when petals are added all around. Be sure to add a stem and leaves to each flower also. Different colored marking pens can be used to make the individual flowers.

These thumbprint pictures can be attractively done on 3-inch by 4½-inch pieces of paper. Then each picture can be backed with a slightly larger piece of construction paper to form a colorful border.

Art Festival

An art festival is a good project for the middle or end of the year. Various art pictures that the children have worked on as a part of their lessons can be displayed in the hallway for all to admire. Children like to see their work appreciated.

Each picture can be backed with colorful construction paper. The child's name should be on each picture. One picture or project of every child in the program should be displayed. Each class or grade level can be assigned a different theme to display a topic they have been studying.

The week before the festival a note can be sent home to the children's families inviting them to come to the art festival. This way the families will allow time before or after class to see the various artistic endeavors. The children can proudly show their parents and siblings the picture they did. Each area where a class's art work is shown should be clearly marked so that it is easy to find.

This type of project builds a positive self-concept in children because they can see that other people admire their abilities and efforts. It makes them feel important to be part of such an undertaking.

Name Decorating

Let the children print their names in large letters on individual sheets of manilla construction paper. Then ask the children to use their imaginations to decorate their names in a special way with crayons.

Names are important to children because they are so closely tied to their self-image. This can be a fun activity. The letter "i" can be dotted with a heart. A letter "o" might become a smile face. Encourage the children to be creative. This activity makes the children feel proud of their names and proud of themselves. The finished pictures make a wonderful bulletin board display.

Listening Time

We need to communicate our acceptance of children by listening attentively to them when they speak. We need to encourage them to share their thoughts, ideas, and opinions. Children need the opportunity to express themselves and know that they will be heard.

We can provide a listening time at the beginning of each class for the children to relate what is happening in their lives. This might be anything from a new puppy to a trip or a visit from grandparents. It builds self-esteem for the children to be listened to with respect by their teachers and classmates. It tells the children that it is okay to be who they are. The language of acceptance is a powerful communication tool for teachers.

Children need to know that we accept them as they are with any imperfections they might have. Only then can they begin to develop their potential. Only then can they become the people that God created them to be. We must be willing to allow children to be themselves.

We must learn to really listen to children when they speak and not just hear them. Children need to feel special. We need to praise their accomplishments. We need to take pride in them so that they will learn to take pride in themselves. Children are a gift to us from God that should be treasured.

chapter 3

Building Community in the Classroom

An important part of the learning process is to build a sense of community among the children in the classroom. The students must feel comfortable with their peers if they are to feel free to participate in class discussions and offer opinions. Children need to be at ease with one another if they are to work together on class activities.

In order to build community, the teachers must set the example by being good listeners and encouraging the children to do the same. Children are more likely to open up and share feelings if they know that they will be listened to with respect by their teachers and fellow students.

Children need to feel that they are a part of things. We need to encourage a sense of belonging in the classroom. This means helping children to discover that they are important to the class. A sense of class spirit helps foster the desire to learn.

Children can learn from one another's ideas and experiences. Students learn more in classrooms where they share ideas with one another as well as the teachers. This interaction with one another multiplies the opportunity for learning. In a sense each child becomes a teacher of the others. The classroom should be a place where students help each other learn and grow.

In the book *First Things,* Rod Brownfield expresses the need for the teacher to help the children learn from one another. He says, "The teacher cannot impose learning; he must create a situation where learning is possible, where students actively participate and share— even create—experiences. Students must interact with peers as well as with the teacher."[1]

[1] Rod Brownfield, *First Things: A Handbook for Beginners in Religious Education* (Dayton, Oh.: Pflaum Press, 1973) p. 31. Used by permission of Pflaum Press.

It is especially important to build community in the religious education classroom. There children learn about such concepts as family of God and caring about others. It is difficult to teach about brotherhood in a room full of strangers.

If a classroom is a faith community that learns together and shares experiences, the students will feel a positive relationship toward one another. This relationship can, hopefully in time, be expanded to include a sense of responsibility for the world community. The experience of a caring classroom community can help the children understand what it means to be part of the Christian community.

Following are some ways to build community in the classroom.

Get Acquainted Games

At the beginning of the year the children need help in getting to know one another. Young children enjoy games that help them learn one another's names in a fun way.

The beanbag game begins with all the children standing in a circle. The teacher throws a beanbag to one of the children. If that child's name is Nancy, she says "I'm Nancy and I'm special." Then she throws the beanbag back to the teacher. Then the teacher throws it to another child until each has had a turn. This game not only helps the children identify the other children by name, but helps them feel important.

Beanbags can be made easily and inexpensively out of two squares of fabric sewn together and filled with dried beans from the grocery store. A large ball that is easy to catch can also be used for this activity.

Another way of introducing the children to one another is the "Hello Game." The children go around the circle and introduce themselves. After each child's name is given, all the children say hello and the name. If the first child's name is Steve, he says, "My name is Steve." Then all the children in unison say "Hello, Steve." This game really makes the children feel welcome and brings many smiles.

Introductions

Older children can be paired off to introduce each other. This is more interesting than introducing oneself year after year. It also guarantees that each child meets at least one other person.

The teacher assigns each child a partner. The children are given five minutes to find out the name of their partner and two things about that child. When the five minutes are up, each child takes a turn introducing another child and telling about that child's hobbies, interests, pets, or whatever.

Introducing the Program

Children need to know what they will be doing in class and what will be expected of them. This is especially important with young children who have had little or no classroom experience.

On the first day of class teachers should explain what topics the children will be studying. The teachers can tell them that they will be learning about God's love for them, the world He made, and how we are to love others. Any specific goals for the year should be outlined.

Learning activities in which the children will be expected to participate should be discussed. The children want to know what they will be doing. Telling about the highlights of the year ahead also helps students look forward to coming to class. Let the children ask questions. They may be very concerned about something that was not mentioned.

If possible, it is a good idea to send a letter to each child before the school year begins explaining that year's program. It also helps the children to feel that they are important. A letter makes the beginning of the year get off to a good start. The children like to know that their teachers are looking forward to getting to know them. The letter can also contain information about the teacher.

Questionnaires

We can help the children in the class become friends by learning about one another. Questionnaires are good for older children. Provide space for them to fill in the blanks with information about themselves.

Questions such as the following allow the children to tell facts about themselves:

1. My name is _____.

2. I am _____ years old.

3. My birthday is on _____.

4. The street I live on is _____.

5. My favorite color is _____.

6. My favorite thing to do is _____.

7. My favorite food is _____.

8. I go to _____ school.

9. My favorite game is _____.

10. My favorite part of the summer was _____.

When the children come into class the following time, the questionnaires can be posted on the bulletin board under an appropriate title such as "Who's Who in Our Class." Be sure that the children know that the answers to the questions will be seen by all.

Pictures of the individual children can be posted with the questionnaires also. This will help the children match faces and names. The children can be asked to bring pictures from home. Some teachers like to take pictures of each child with an instant camera.

This information helps the children to find out facts about each other. It helps friendships form when children discover common interests about which they can talk. Studying the display is a good before-class activity for children who arrive early.

Friendship Chains

This is a fun project that requires the children to work together. It encourages a spirit of friendship among the children. A friendship chain requires the cooperation of all the children.

The children print their names on individual strips of paper approximately 11½ inches long by 1 inch wide. Then the children loop the strips together to form an interlocking chain (see illustration). The chain can be strung across the ceiling or the bulletin board.

The chain can be made longer by giving each child several strips of paper. If the class is small, each child can have a different color of

Figure 3-1. Friendship Chain.

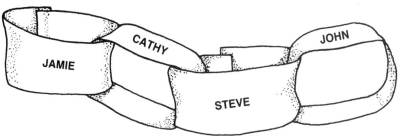

paper. All the children's names strung together in a friendship chain symbolize their friendship with one another. It is a colorful and meaning-ful way of decorating the classroom.

Name Game

A fun name review is the name game for children. This activity helps the children remember one another's names. It also helps the children feel that they are part of the class.

The teacher describes the children in the class one at a time. The other children must guess the name of the child being described. A description might be "I see someone with red hair and pigtails who is wearing a blue dress. Who is it?" The children look around to see who it could be. The game continues until all the children have been guessed.

A similar name game for older children uses written descriptions. Short descriptions of each child can be written on pieces of paper by the students themselves. They could be limited to three sentences such as "I am a girl. I play soccer. I like rainbows." Then all the pieces of paper are put into a coffee can.

Each child can take a turn to pick out a description and read it to the class. All the children can guess who it is. This is a good activity because it involves the children themselves at every step of the way.

Tape Recording

Children can learn about one another through a tape recording of the class. The teacher can act like an interviewer on a television talk show. Each child can be interviewed. Questions can be asked such as name, family members, pets, favorite activities, age, hobbies, favorite television show, and favorite place to visit.

When the tape is completed, it can be played back for the class. This activity helps the children learn about the likes and interests of others. It also makes them feel special to have been interviewed on tape. Everyone likes to hear themselves. This idea previously appeared in my article "Building Community in the Classroom", which was published in *Religion Teacher's Journal.*[2]

[2]Previously published in *Religion Teacher's Journal* (October 1984) published by Twenty-Third Publications, P.O. Box 180, Mystic, CT 06355. Used by permission.

Tree Banner

A good way to help all the children feel that they belong is through the making of a class banner with each child's name. Each year a different theme can be used. Banners can be made by individual classes. This activity can be most effective, however, if all the students in the program contribute to the banner as a sign of community. The banner can be placed in the hallway where the children will see it each time they come to class.

One tree with many leaves bearing the individual children's names makes a wonderful banner. A brown trunk and branches can be painted on white cloth. A tree can also be made out of posterboard with brown for the trunk and green for the top.

The children can print their names on individual paper leaves and put them on the branches with double-stick tape (see illustration). Younger children can use precut leaves. Older children should cut out

Figure 3-2. Tree Banner.

their own leaves so that they can make them unique. The children should choose which color leaves they want. Red, yellow, brown, and orange make a colorful fall tree.

In the springtime the children can replace the fall leaves with green name leaves as a sign of growth and hope. This keeps the spirit of belonging alive throughout the year.

Tree Planting

A project that all the children in the class work on together builds community. Such a project is planting a live tree. The children have tangible proof of what they can accomplish when they work together. Each class or day or age group can plant their own tree.

Holes for the trees should be dug ahead of time in a suitable place on the church lawn. The trees should be unwrapped or unpotted in advance also. The children can talk about trees in their classrooms. They can discuss various ways that trees are useful. They provide food such as apples and pecans. They are homes for birds. They give shade on a hot day. They are beautiful to look at with all their green leaves. They provide wood and paper. The children can also talk about what all living things need to grow—sunshine and water.

The tree planting hopefully will take place on a sunny day. The teacher or program director can begin the ceremony by placing the tree in the hole with these words, "We plant this tree today as a sign of God's creation." Then the children can throw paper cups full of dirt into the hole. Some of the classes should be assigned to water the tree with plastic cups. A bucket of water is necessary in which to dunk them. This way all the children have a hand in planting the tree.

Then the children can be directed to join hands and form a circle around the tree. They can say a prayer of thanks to God for trees. Put a weatherproof sign in front of the tree on a small stake telling who planted it and the date.

Each time the children see the tree growing, they can feel a sense of pride in what they did together.

Class Discussion

Students need the opportunity to learn from one another. They should be encouraged to participate in class discussions and share information, ideas, opinions, and experiences.

Teachers can help promote this sharing through effective questioning. Questions that call for a "yes" or "no" answer should be avoided. Instead, questions should be asked that require the students to think.

In *Teacher Improvement: Practice, Study,* Locke E. Bowman, Jr. states that effective questions can be divided into three levels:

> Many questions we ask are about students' KNOWLEDGE—facts, data, information. These begin with *Who? What? When? Where?*
>
> A next level of questioning has to do with *ANALYSIS* of data. When we search for insight into meanings, seek to clarify, or consider how ideas relate to one another, we probe more deeply by asking *Why?* and *How?*
>
> Finally, we use questions to encourage personal *EVALUATION*. What are the students' opinions, their stances, in relation to ideas and issues? These are questions that begin: *What do you think about . . . ?* Or, *What can we do about . . . ?*[3]

These types of questions lead to learning. They encourage children to talk and to share ideas.

It is also very important that students be encouraged to ask questions themselves about things that puzzle them. In order to foster student questions, the classroom must be a place where students know their questions will be welcome and considered seriously. Students will closely observe the teacher's attitude toward those who ask questions. If the questions are brushed aside to get on with the lesson, the children will think, "What's the use?" If the teacher treats questions in a condescending manner, no student will risk feeling foolish to ask a question.

In the article "Questions: Directions for Growth" in *Catechist* magazine, Patrick Kirk states the importance of student's questions in religious education:

> Genuine faith is such a personal creation that it will not grow unless a person is encouraged to be a challenger and questioner and a searcher for answers. Questions received in an atmosphere of openness and affirmation can lay the basis for developing the confidence to continue asking, intelligent and purposeful searching, and growing.[4]

---

[3]Locke E. Bowman, Jr., *Teacher Improvement: Practice, Study* (Scottsdale, Ariz.: The Arizona Experiment, 1976), p. IV-I. Used by permission of the National Teacher Education Program.

[4]Patrick Kirk, "Questions: Directions for Growth," *Catechist,* vol 14, no. 5 (February 1981), p. 6. Used by permission of publisher, Peter Li, Inc.

Children's questions deserve answers. Through questions the students grow in faith. Their questions help make the lesson part of their lives. If their questions are answered, they will hopefully set a pattern of searching for answers throughout their lives.

Small Groups

A great deal of learning can take place using small groups in the classroom. The children can be divided into groups and assigned a topic. The findings of each group can be summarized and presented to the class.

It is important to choose a fair method of assigning students to their various groups. It is advisable not to let students pick their own groups. No one wants to be the last one chosen. Children can instead be divided by the first letter of their names. For two groups all the students A-M can be in one group and N-Z in another. For several smaller groups the children can count off one, two, three, four, five. All those with numbers alike are in the same group.

Many types of projects can be done successfully in small groups. The research project works well. For example, each group can be assigned a saint or Bible figure. Easy-to-read children's books should be available to the children with information about the individuals assigned. Each of the children in the group can contribute to the report. A spokesperson should be chosen for the group by the children.

Books on signs and symbols should be included to help each group choose an appropriate symbol for the person they are researching. This symbol should be drawn on posterboard by the group as something their person represents.

Then each leader can present the group's report to the class. The symbol poster should be displayed while the speaker tells the class about the saint or Bible person. The poster gives the children a visual symbol that helps them remember the information that they hear given in the report.

Children learn by being involved. In small groups they have more of an opportunity to talk than in a classroom full of students. Small groups also give the students a variety of people from whom they can learn. Small groups can be a valuable way for students to gain information and to learn from one another. It also helps them learn to work together. Small groups give the students the opportunity to unite and work toward a common goal.

We Follow Jesus Banner

Children need to understand that we are all members of God's family. We are all to follow Jesus' Gospel message of love together. We are to live His words in all that we do. Young children can more readily comprehend this idea of working together to follow Jesus through making a "We Follow Jesus Banner."

A colorful bulletin board can be used for the background for this project. Cut letters that say "We Follow Jesus" out of different colors of construction paper. Pin them to the bulletin board.

The children can stand on pieces of construction paper and trace the shape of their feet. Then they should put their names on their footprints in black marker to identify them. The footprints are then cut out. Younger children will need help.

In a small class, the children can trace and cut out both feet. With a large class, half the children can trace their left foot and half can trace their right foot. The children should use various colors of construction paper to make a colorful banner.

The children can pin their footprints on the bulletin board under the theme words. One footprint should be placed slightly ahead of the other in the pair so that the footprints look like they are walking (see illustration).

Explain to the children that the footprints symbolize that we are walking in Jesus' footprints. We are trying to follow His teachings. This

Figure 3-3. We Follow Jesus Banner.

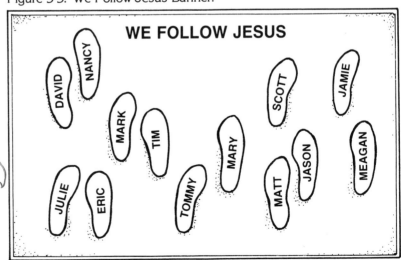

puts an abstract idea into an understandable form. This idea comes from *Living in God's Love* by Jeanne Coolahan Mueller.[5]

Class Mural

Working together on a class mural can help young children get to know one another. Sharing space and crayons teaches cooperation. Murals can be drawn on end rolls of newsprint available from many newspapers at a nominal cost. These wide rolls can be cut off at any length suitable to the number of children in the class or the display space available.

The mural idea is a learning activity that can be adapted to many lessons. A great mural is one that can be titled "God Loves Us All" across the top. The children each draw a picture of themselves with crayons or markers and sign their names. This is a good learning experience for young children. The finished mural should be displayed on the bulletin board or on the wall for all to admire.

Class Newspaper

Older children can learn about one another through making a class newspaper. This can be a one-time project with articles about individual class members, teachers, class projects, and other class activities. Spring is a good time to compile a newspaper because the children will have months of classes about which to write.

Students can be assigned to work together on short articles. If possible, the articles can be typed by a volunteer in columns and pasted up to look like the front page of a newspaper. Each article should have a headline written by the authors. Then the newspaper can be duplicated for the children to take home. This provides a great sense of accomplishment and a great review. Projects such as this instill a sense of class pride and community.

[5]Jeanne Coolahan Mueller, *Living in God's Love,* Vacation Bible School Series Planning Guide (Minneapolis, Minn.: Augsburg Publishing House, 1981), p. 22. Used by permission of Augsburg Publishing House.

chapter 4

Discovering God's Creation

Children have an inborn sense of wonder and awe at the world around them. We can enable children to see through creation the evidence of God's love for them. We can help them learn about the joy of God's love through exploring the endless variety in nature. We can nurture their understanding of God by helping them to learn about His creation.

We need to enable children to appreciate God's gifts—the uniqueness of each person, the warmth of sunshine, the vastness of an ocean made up of tiny drops of water. Through the world in which they live, we can help the children discover God's presence in their lives.

To children the world is an exciting adventure. Everything is new as they see it for the first time. They are eager to learn about the world around them. We can encourage this curiosity and use it to help the children experience God's love.

The creation story can give children a foundation for faith in God all their lives. Because we can see evidence of God's love everywhere, we know that He is here around us always. We know that He will always be here just as we know that He will always send the dawn after the night.

The wonders of nature are always changing. There is always something new to discover. Creation is a great teaching tool for children because they can experience it in their own lives.

Following are some ways we can help children to discover God's presence in their lives through the wonders of creation.

Creation Story

Read or tell the children the marvelous story of creation from the Bible (Genesis 1:1-31, 2:1-3). It is a fascinating account of how God made the world out of nothing. The children will be amazed to learn that before God made the world there was no light, no animals, no people.

We need to stress to the children that everything God made is good. Explain that God saved the best thing for last to create—people. Tell the children how our world is a gift from God because He loves us.

Encourage the children to name things that God made such as flowers, mountains, people, animals, rivers, trees. This gives children the opportunity to think about the creation story and contribute to the class discussion.

Explain to the children that there are some things that God did not make directly, but that He gave man the ability and materials to make. Houses are an example. God gave us trees for wood, hands that can build, and a mind to think of the idea of a house in which to live.

Through the story of God's creation the children will begin to learn how the world came to be. They will begin to understand the depth of God's love for His people.

Nature Walk

Take the children outside on a nature walk on the church grounds for a first-hand look at the beauty and wonder of nature. Walk at a leisurely pace so that the children have the opportunity to see the different kinds of things that God has made.

Let the children enjoy the warmth of the sun and the sounds of the birds chirping. Point out to them the variety of plants, flowers, and trees that God has made. Each is unique in its own way. Encourage them to look for ladybugs on leaves and squirrels in trees. Ask them to touch the rough bark of a tree and to smell a flower. Let them discover God's world for themselves. The sense of wonder is a great teaching tool.

When the children come back inside, let them talk about their experiences and ask questions. In this way they will learn to interpret what they experienced on their walk. Explain to them that we know that God is here around us because we see evidence of His creation everywhere.

Creation Art

Encourage the children to draw their favorite thing that God made with crayons, markers, or watercolors. Artistic expression is an important part of the learning process for children. They must think about what they have learned before they can translate it onto the paper in front of them. Learning is such an individual process that each person must decide what is the most important part of the lesson.

Art allows children to express themselves in a way that is not limited by their language ability. Children may not always be able to find the words to express themselves, but they can put their feelings and ideas down on paper.

Art allows the children the freedom to experience what they are learning in a personally meaningful way. Also art allows them the opportunity to use their God-given artistic ability to express themselves. Remember that it is the learning that takes place through art that is important, not the outcome of the finished product.

Creation Banners

Banners are a colorful way of expressing the meaning of a lesson without the use of words. They can be used to help the children learn about God's creation. Children enjoy making banners. This activity helps them remember what they have learned.

Individual creation banners can be made from pieces of burlap. The top of each banner should be hemmed before class. A 10-inch wide by 15-inch long banner is a good size for children to make. A 12-inch wooden dowel can be threaded through the top of each banner. The ends of the dowel can be tied with lengths of green yarn to make a hanger.

Green rickrack can be used to divide the banner into four sections. One piece should be glued horizontally and one piece vertically. Felt shapes can be glued onto the banner to represent the various things that God has made. In one section can be the shape of a person cut from blue felt. In another area can be a bright yellow sun. In another section the children can glue a green tree with a brown trunk. A tulip cut from red felt can be glued in another section with a green felt stem and leaves (see illustration).

The children will be very proud to take these banners home. Every time they look at their banners they will be reminded that God made our world. This type of learning by doing reinforces what is taught. This banner idea was previously published in my article "Vacation Bible School" in *Catechist* magazine.[1]

---

[1] This idea originally appeared in *Catechist* (February 1983) and is used here by permission of the publisher, Peter Li, Inc., 2451 East River Road, Dayton, Ohio 45439.

Figure 4-1. Creation Banner.

Nature Table

A nature table gives the children a close-up look at nature and the things that God made. Display various objects and provide inexpensive magnifying glasses so that the children can examine details. Encourage the children to handle the nature objects.

Ask the children to help with this project also. They can bring in items from their yards. This will provide a wide variety of nature objects. Items such as the following are good for a nature table:

Pinecones	Flowers
Rocks	Acorns
Shells	Tree bark
Leaves	

This is also a good activity for early arrivals. They can work individually looking at things before class begins.

Creation Matching Cards

A fun learning activity for young children is creation matching cards. It helps them remember things that God has made. This activity reinforces the creation lesson and makes learning interesting for the children.

Prepare matching cards for the children with index cards and self-stick seals. These seals are available in card shops and come with pictures of the sun, a butterfly, a squirrel, a turtle, flowers, leaves, and others.

Draw a line vertically down the middle of each index card. On the left side place a seal. Leave the right side blank (see illustration). Then prepare the matching cards by cutting another group of index cards in half vertically. On each half card put one of the seals.

Explain to the children that they can match up things that God has made. The children can pair up the cards by placing the matching picture on the larger card. Any number of children can work on this activity at the same time around a table.

This activity is a challenge to young children, but well within the realm of their capabilities. They will feel proud of themselves for being able to complete this activity. Creation matching cards encourage the children to learn by doing. They become familiar with things that God made for us. This is a great activity for young children because it does

Figure 4-2. Creation Matching Card.

not involve reading. It is good for children who arrive early for class because they can do it by themselves. Store the cards in a pencil box with a hinged lid.

Planting Seeds

Planting seeds is a wonderful way for children to experience the miracle of creation firsthand. Explain to the children that God gave us seeds so that we would always have plants and flowers. Each new plant gives more seeds so that the cycle of life can be continued. Children will be amazed to learn that even the mighty oak tree grows from a small acorn.

Show the children how to plant seeds in paper drinking cups. Fill the cups about three-fourths full with potting soil. Provide fast-growing marigold or zinnia seeds for the children to push into the soil. Several seeds should be planted in each cup because not every seed will grow.

Provide poems and popsickle sticks. The children can cut out the poems and tape them onto the popsickle sticks. A poem such as the following can be used:

> I planted a seed
> and here it will grow.
> It will become a flower
> because God made it so.

Push the popsickle stick into the dirt inside the back rim of the cup. Thus, the growing plant will be visible in front of the sign. Explain to the children how to care for their plants. Plants need sunshine and water to grow. Caution the children against giving their plants too much water.

What a thrill it is in a couple of days when a little seedling appears. It makes the children feel important to be a part of God's plan for continuing creation.

Colors

Children can learn a great deal about God's creation through the study of His gift of colors. Colors make our world a bright and beautiful place to be. The study of colors is especially good for young children because they can see colors all around them.

Talk to the children about the various colors that God made. Hold up a sheet of colored paper and ask the children to name that color.

Then let them think of things that God made of that color. Teachers should also contribute their ideas. Go through all the colors in this way.

For green the children might name grass and frogs. Yellow is the color of lemons and dandelions. Blue is the color of the sky and blueberries. For purple the children might think of violets and plums. Brown is the color of robins and dirt. Gray is for rocks and elephants. Black is the color of blackbirds and horses. Orange is the color of oranges and butterflies. For red the children may name apples and cherries.

A fun follow-up activity is to show the children how to make a colorful mosaic by tearing one-inch or smaller squares of construction paper. The pieces can be glued overlapping one another on another sheet of construction paper.

Younger children find joy and satisfaction in making an abstract design that is all their own. Older children can shape theirs into a colorful rainbow or other object. These pictures turn out surprisingly well. It is interesting to see the pictures taking shape out of the arrangement of bits of colored paper. This activity helps the children to appreciate God's gift of colors.

Candy Cup Flowers

Children enjoy making craft projects. They learn by doing. One creation craft project children like is candy cup flower pictures.

For the background each child can use a half sheet of blue construction paper. At the bottom of each paper they should put "God made the flowers." Then they can cut out stems and leaves for two flowers from green construction paper. Next each child can cut out a sun from yellow paper. The stems, leaves, and sun should be glued to each child's paper. To have their flowers bloom, the children can glue on small candy cups available from kitchen supply stores. This creates a three-dimensional look.

The children will be pleased to take home their projects to display. Each time they look at their pictures, they will be reminded of what they learned in class.

Clay Dough

Clay dough is wonderful for children because it allows freedom of expression. Creativity is a God-given talent that we need to encourage in children. Children have the potential for creative expression if teachers provide the opportunity and the encouragement.

To make clay dough mix 4 cups of flour, 2 cups of salt, and enough water to make the mixture pliable. Food coloring can be added to make it colorful. Store in an airtight container.

The children can shape animals, people, or whatever they wish. The dough can be used over and over so that each child can make several things. The possibilities are limited only by their imaginations.

Animals

Children like to learn about animals. The best learning comes from real animals. Sometimes church members raise animals that can be brought to the classroom for the children to pet and to hold. This interaction with an animal helps the children learn more about animals than anything else. Rabbits are good classroom visitors. They are fun to watch as they hop and cuddly to pet.

Pictures of various animals that God made can help children learn about the variety of animals. Children's nature magazines are a good source of pictures of penguins, monkeys, bears, camels, and giraffes. Tell the children about what these animals eat, where they live, and how big they are.

An assortment of pictures of animals can also be laid out on a table. Let each child choose a picture of an animal. Then each child can be given the opportunity to tell the class about that animal. This allows the children to participate in the lesson and to learn from one another.

Young children enjoy imitating animals. They can make the sounds that animals make. It is also fun for them to act like various animals. Ask the children to perform actions such as the following:

> Waddle like a duck
> Gallop like a horse
> Hop like a rabbit
> Fly like a bird
> Walk like an elephant
> Jump like a kangaroo
> Swim like a fish

Children learn through what they do. They learn through being involved personally in the lesson.

Guessing Game

An animal guessing game is fun for young children. It helps reinforce the idea that God made the animals. Ask the following riddles and let the children guess which animal is being described.

I have big ears.
I am gray.
I have a trunk.
God made me. Who am I? (elephant)

I have four legs and a tail.
I can swim.
I carry my house on my back.
God made me. Who am I? (turtle)

I can hop.
I have big feet.
I have a pouch.
God made me. Who am I? (kangaroo)

I am fuzzy.
I eat leaves.
I turn into a butterfly.
God made me. Who am I? (caterpillar)

I am very tall.
I have a long neck.
I eat leaves from trees.
God made me. Who am I? (giraffe)

Sun Catchers

Sun catchers are a fun craft project for children. The children cut out shapes from black construction paper. Then they cut away the middle section leaving only a frame. A piece of colorful tissue paper is cut in a shape to fit the frame. Then the tissue shape is glued to the back of the frame.

The fish shape makes a great sun catcher. Details can be added to the tissue shape with pieces of black construction paper. For a fish, an eye and fin can be carefully glued in place (see illustration). Explain to the children that not only is the fish something that God created, but it was a sign used by the early Christians. Then the children should punch a hole in the top of each frame and add a yarn hanger.

The sun catchers are hung in a window so that the sunlight can shine through the thin tissue paper for a stained-glass effect. Sun catchers are a way to help children learn about God's world.

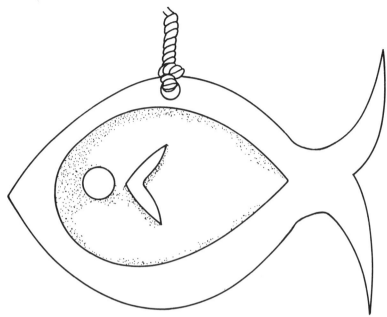

Figure 4-3. Sun Catcher.

Pinecone Birdfeeders

A good project for children to make is pinecone birdfeeders. This helps the children learn about creation. It reminds them that we need to care about God's world and the creatures in it.

Each child can make a birdfeeder by spreading a pinecone with peanut butter. Then each pinecone is rolled in a pie pan filled with birdseed. The birdseed will stick to the peanut butter. Yarn can be tied around the pinecone to use as a hangar. These birdfeeders can be hung from any tree limb. If the children are taking their birdfeeders home to hang, put each birdfeeder in a plastic sandwich bag for the trip. These birdfeeders are safe for birds and ecologically sound.

This is a good opportunity to talk to the children about taking care of our world. Older children will be interested in hearing about projects currently underway such as nature refuges for endangered animals. Thus, future generations will be able to enjoy eagles and other birds and animals threatened with extinction.

Creation Mobiles

Mobiles are fun for children to make and fun to look at later. To make a creation mobile, the children cut shapes out of paper or posterboard of various things that God has made. Each child needs five shapes. These might be a sun, a person, a star, a flower, and a squirrel. Younger children can choose from precut shapes to use. The children need to punch a hole in the top of each creation shape. Then lengths of yarn can be tied to each shape.

A clothes hangar makes a good mobile. The shapes should be tied to the bottom of the hangar at varying lengths (see illustration). The mobiles can be hung at home in a child's room by hooking the top of the hangar over a curtain rod. Every time the children look at their creation mobiles, they will be reminded of some of the things that God made for love of us.

Seasons

The seasons offer a good opportunity to teach children about God. We can help children understand that we know that God is always with us because He always sends spring.

Figure 4-4. Creation Mobile.

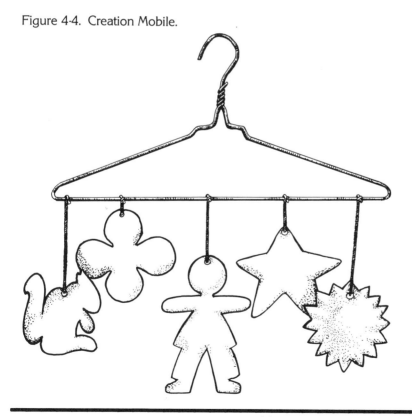

The children can discuss the signs of the various seasons. Fall brings the changing colors of leaves to yellow, red, and orange. In the fall children can rake the leaves into piles and jump into them. School starts and the weather is cooler. See if the children can name other signs of fall.

In winter the trees are bare. Many birds go away to warm climates. The weather is cold and children wear jackets and mittens. In some parts of the country snow falls. Where it gets very cold, children can go ice skating. The children will probably think of other things that happen in the winter.

In the spring there are buds on the trees. We plant seeds. The birds sing. Baby animals are born. Flowers bloom. Children play outside. Spring brings many changes. Some of the children may have noticed them.

In the summer the trees are filled with leaves. Gardens grow. School is out. The weather is hot and sunny. Children can go swimming. The children may do many things over the summer. See how many they can remember.

The children can play a seasons matching game to demonstrate their grasp of information about the seasons. Cut pictures out of magazines that show seasonal activities or nature. Provide four boxes for the children. On each box put the name of the season and a sample picture. Even children too young to read can sort the pictures into the appropriate boxes. Pictures of leaves and pumpkins would go into the fall box. Pictures of mittens and snowmen could be assigned to the winter box. Pictures of budding trees and planting seeds can be placed in the spring box. Pictures of gardens and children swimming would be placed in the summer box.

The children might also like to act out various seasonal activities in a seasons charades game. Each child could have a turn acting out an activity such as swimming or raking leaves or planting seeds or ice skating. The other children in the class can guess to which season the activity belongs. This is another learning activity that does not require reading.

Whatever the season we can celebrate the many gifts that God has given us. God in His wisdom gave us things to look forward to in each change of seasons. Everything we see around us reminds us of God's love for us.

The children can make a book about the seasons to help them remember. Construction paper can be folded in half to form a cover.

White paper can be stapled inside of the book. One page should be labeled "Fall," one "Winter," one "Spring," and another "Summer." On each page the children can draw something appropriate to that season. The book can be titled "God Made the Seasons."

Monkey Puppets

The children will enjoy making monkey puppets to help them remember an animal that God made. The body of the puppet is a brown lunch sack. The children cut out various body pieces from construction paper and glue them to the sack (see illustration). The following pieces are needed for each puppet:

> Fringed brown hair
> Two brown ears
> Two round white eyes
> Two small black eyes
> Two yellow mouth pieces
> One red mouth piece
> One round brown nose
> Two brown arms
> Two brown feet
> One curly brown tail

The lunch sack should be turned upside down. The fringed hair is then glued just behind the top crease of the bag. The ears are glued on either side just behind the front flap. Bend the ears forward after gluing. Then glue on the white eye pieces and the black eye pieces. The inside of the mouth goes under the flap so that it is not seen until the puppet's mouth opens. The two yellow mouth parts are glued next. One piece goes on at the bottom of the flap and the other just beneath the red mouth piece. Then the nose is glued in place.

The body of the puppet is done next. The hands and arms are glued on the front of the puppet's body. Glue about a half inch of the top of the arms and then crease them so that the arms hang down. Glue part of the feet just inside the bottom front edge of the sack. Then bend the feet forward parallel to the ground. The tail is glued last onto the back of the puppet. Glue the tail about an inch and crease the tail so that it sticks out from the back of the puppet.

The children can make their monkeys talk by putting their hands inside the flap of the lunch sack and moving it up and down. When not

Figure 4-5. Monkey Puppet.

being used, the monkey can stand upright alone on a shelf. Simply open the sack and stand the monkey so it balances on its feet and the back edge of the sack. This idea is from the book *Puppet Party* by Goldie Taub Chernoff.[2]

Five Senses

God gave each of us five gifts that we can use to learn about the world He made. All learning takes place through the senses. Through sight,

[2]Scholastic Inc. from excerpts from *Puppet Party* by Goldie Taub Chernoff, pp. 6-7. Copyright © 1971 by Goldie Taub Chernoff. Used by permission.

hearing, taste, touch, and smell we can discover the wonders of creation around us.

We can foster an appreciation of the five senses by helping the children become aware of how much our senses enrich our lives. We need to provide opportunities in the classroom for the children to explore their five senses. Even young children enjoy learning about their senses because it is within the realm of their experience.

Have the children think of ways in which we use each sense:

We use our eyes to see many things all around us—the people we love, birds flying in the sky, flowers blooming, the wide variety of colors in nature, the smile of a friend, or a squirrel climbing up a tree.

We use our ears to hear many different sounds—the voices of our families and friends, music and laughter, the sound of a waterfall, the chirps of birds early in the morning, the bark of a pet dog, or the rustling of leaves high up in a tree.

We use our mouths to taste our food—the cold glass of milk, the sweet taste of fresh strawberries, hot bread fresh from the oven, or the tangy taste of lemonade.

We use our noses to smell our world—the aroma of cookies baking, the sweet fragrance of flowers, the sharp tang of smoke, the smell of a skunk, or the damp smell after it has rained.

We use our sense of touch all the time—to hug a parent, to feel the roughness of tree bark, to feel the softness of a kitten, to warn us not to pick up something hot, or to help those around us. The sense of touch is so important in our lives in many ways.

One activity that uses all the five senses is making popcorn. Using an electric popcorn popper in the classroom, the children can see the popcorn kernels popping, smell it all through the room, and hear the popping sounds. Then, best of all, they will be able to touch and taste it.

It is important to help the children explore the wonders of creation with their senses. In this way they will come to know God's presence in their lives.

chapter 5

Encouraging Children to Care

Caring is an important part of what it means to live as a Christian. Being a Christian should make a difference in our lives. As Jesus said, "By this love you have for one another everyone will know that you are my disciples" (John 13:35).

We are our brothers' keepers. We need to care about people and what happens to them. This does not apply just to our families and friends. We also need to care about and help people in our local community and in the world.

We must help the children learn to care about others. We must enable them to discover ways they are called by God's love to lead Christian lives every day.

Children must learn that they are loved by God and that God wants them to extend that love to others. Children learn about loving through being loved. We must help them live as members of God's family.

The result of religious teaching should not be a mastery of facts, but the acquiring of a caring attitude toward others. To help the children achieve this goal, we must guide them in exploring ways of helping others. We must help them to try out these ideas in the classroom. The children must decide the ways they will use to care about others. They must be encouraged to make caring a part of their daily lives.

We also must provide role models. Children need people to provide examples of ways they can continue to care throughout their lives.

Encouraging children to care about others is an important part of religious education. Following are some ways to do this.

Friendly Actions

We can begin with young children by helping them learn what are friendly actions and what are not. A good activity to help children learn about being friendly begins with a list of friendly and unfriendly actions. Each statement should then be put on a separate index card. The cards can be put in the middle of a circle of children sitting on the floor.

First discuss with the children what it means to be friendly. Then divide the children sitting next to each other into teams of two. Have each team choose a card from the pile. The statements will need to be read for the younger children. Older children can take turns reading the cards out loud to the class.

Each team should take turns telling if their statement describes a way to be friendly. If the team decides that the action is unfriendly, they should tell the class why they think so. Then the team should change the sentence for the class so that it describes a friendly action.

Some actions that can be used include the following:

> Someone smiles at you.
> A classmate tells you he doesn't like you.
> A friend tells you that he likes your drawing.
> A person tells you that she doesn't want to sit by you.
> A classmate helps you with a puzzle.
> Someone plays a game with you.
> A friend calls you a bad name.
> A classmate helps you pick up the crayons you dropped.

This activity was developed by Michele and Craig Borba in their book *Self-Esteem: A Classroom Affair.*[1]

Smile Badges

We can help the children understand that their actions affect others. Explain to the children that if they are cross, that makes the people around them cross. Then those people might be mean to other people who pass the bad feelings along. Point out that the reverse is also true. If they smile at other people, those people might smile at others. Thus, good feelings will spread.

---

[1] From *Self-Esteem: A Classroom Affair,* by Michele and Craig Borba. Copyright © 1978 Michele and Craig Borba, p. 56. Published by Winston Press, Inc., 430 Oak Grove, Minneapolis, MN 55403. All rights reserved. Used with permission.

Figure 5-1. Smile Badge.

Show the children how to make bright yellow smile badges to wear. They can cut four-inch circles out of yellow construction paper. If they need a circle pattern, they can draw around a wide cup turned upside down. Then they can use black markers to add two large eyes and a big smile (see illustration). Double-stick tape will allow the children to wear the smile badges home as a reminder to them and others to smile.

Pictures

Pictures are an indispensible teaching tool. Pictures can teach children many things that words cannot. Pictures can appeal to the emotions. They can help children understand abstract concepts such as love, understanding, helping, and caring. Pictures can help children learn about others.

Pictures of people are great discussion starters for children because they motivate thinking. They provide a common basis for discussion among the children. Pictures help children learn values.

A picture of a parent reading to a child can help children learn about the love of their parents and of the God who made all things. A picture of a child hitting another child can lead to a discussion of feelings. A picture of children laughing can help children understand about forgiveness and peace. A picture of one child pulling another in a wagon can help the children discuss caring. A picture of an elderly person sitting alone can lead to a discussion of our attitudes and actions toward older people. A picture of a handicapped child can help children learn to accept all people.

Pictures are a great way to introduce new concepts to the children. Teachers can get the discussion started by asking appropriate questions such as:

> Who do you think these people might be?
> What are these people doing?
> How do you think that they feel?
> How would you change this picture?
> Did anything like this ever happen to you?
> How did you handle the situation?

Children's Books

Books are an important educational tool for teachers of religious education. Books speak the language of children. Books help children understand.

Books meet many needs of children. They help children learn about themselves, their world, and others. Children by their very nature are me-centered. Books help children to discover how others feel and to put themselves in the place of others. Books help the children to see how their actions affect other people.

Books can appeal to children's emotions. Children can relate to books. In her book *How to Be a Very, Very, Very, Very Good Catechist,* Margaret Timmerman, M.H.S.H. states: "Authentic stories capture a slice of life, an event of human interest, and express it in a way that challenges, threatens, amuses, excites, motivates, or in some manner moves the affectivity of the listener . . ."[2]

Simple books that the children can readily understand and follow are the best. Keep the age of the listeners in mind. The story should relate to the everyday experiences of the children.

Follow the book with discussion. Allow the children to tell of similar things that happened to them. Encourage their ideas and opinions.

---

[2]Margaret Timmerman, M.H.S.H., *How to Be a Very, Very, Very, Very Good Catechist* (Mystic, Conn.: Twenty-Third Publications, 1981), p. 81. Used by permission of Twenty-Third Publications.

Listening Tapes

Children need experience in determining ways in which they might help other people in their lives. One way to help them learn is to pose problem situations for them. Then they can respond with their own ideas. Help them decide. There may be more than one good suggestion for each situation.

One way to do this in the classroom is to tape record several problem situations for the children. Play the tape and let them hear the problem. Then they can discuss what might be done about each situation. This is an especially good method for children who are not good readers.

This is a good project for an older class to do for a younger class. The older class can think up dilemmas and tape record them. Several situations should be put on each tape.

Some ideas that can be used for the listening tape are the following:

A little girl named Sally knocked over her mother's vase and broke it. Sally's mom thinks that Sally's younger brother did it and he has to stay in his room the rest of the day. If Sally tells her mom that she broke the vase, her mom will not let her have a friend sleep overnight. Sally's little brother is always teasing her so she doesn't really feel sorry for him. What should Sally do?

A little boy named Ben lives two houses away from an older woman named Mrs. Murphy. Mrs. Murphy has three grown children and five grandchildren, but they all live far away. Mrs. Murphy is always calling to Ben when he walks by her house to play baseball with his friends. Sometimes she just talks to him. Other times she asks him to mail a letter. Ben doesn't like to stop because he knows that his friends are waiting for him. What should Ben do?

Cathy has a friend named Lisa. Lisa broke her arm and has to stay in the hospital for a week. Then she has to stay at home for two more weeks. Lisa can't go to school or Brownie meetings. What can Cathy do for Lisa?

Steve is walking down the hall after religious education classes. His dad calls to him to hurry. Steve is going to a birthday party that starts in 15 minutes. Steve hears a noise and turns around. Alan, one of his classmates, has dropped his papers, book, and crayons all over the floor. Should Steve pretend he hasn't seen or go back and help?

A little girl named Jennifer is playing with her friend, Kelly. They have just started a game of Monopoly. Just then the little girl from across the street rings the doorbell. She wants to know if Jennifer can play. Jennifer sees Kelly shaking her head no. What should Jennifer say?

A little boy named Larry has a sister named Julie. Julie's best friend went camping with her family and won't be back for a week. Julie can't find anyone with whom to play. What can Larry do to cheer up Julie?

Situations such as these encourage children to think. The children have the opportunity to learn from one another as they discuss possible ideas. The teacher's guidance and experience in dealing with such matters also helps them to learn and grow.

Happy Day Cards

The children can have fun making cards to give to people whose days need brightening. Discuss with the children to whom they might give their cards. People such as parents, relatives, neighbors, pastors, or other children could be named.

Ask the children how they feel when someone gives cards to them. Do they feel happy? Do they feel excited? Do they get a good feeling inside? Ask them how they think the people who receive their cards will feel.

Construction paper folded in half widthwise can be used for the cards. The front can be decorated with paper shapes cut out of contrasting colors of paper. Flowers are always a cheerful choice of patterns to glue on the front of cards (see illustration).

Figure 5-2. Happy Day Card.

Inside each card the children can print the words "Have a happy day" and then sign their names. Young children will need to have the words printed for them.

Happy day cards always seem to provide a good feeling for the givers as well as the recipients.

Helpers Game

Children come only gradually to an awareness of others. We need to help them know that there are people in their lives who love them and care for them. Children learn kindness through people who are kind to them.

Young children like to play guessing games. They feel proud of themselves when they guess the right answer. A guessing game of helpers helps them learn about people in their lives who help them.

Questions such as the following can be asked:

I'm thinking of someone who takes care of us when we are sick. Who is it? (Doctor, nurse, parent).

I'm thinking of someone who reads to you and tucks you in at night. Who is it? (Parent, grandparent)

I'm thinking of someone who brings our mail. Who is it? (Mailman)

I'm thinking of someone who helps us learn about God. Who it is? (Teacher, pastor, parent)

I'm thinking of someone who fights fires. Who is it? (Fireman)

I'm thinking of someone who loves us all the time, no matter what. Who is it? (God, parent)

Good Samaritan

Teachers are mediators between God and man. We have the responsibility and joy of helping children learn about love. We are to pass on to the next generation the message that God wants us to love others.

We need to help children learn and understand Jesus' words ". . . You must love your neighbor as yourself" (Matthew 22:39). When Jesus was asked about who is considered our neighbor, He told His listeners the parable of the Good Samaritan (Luke 10:30-37). This is a good story to read or tell to the children. It puts an abstract concept into a concrete and understandable form.

The children can discuss the story guided by questions. They can talk about why the Good Samaritan stopped and why the others didn't. They can discuss how the traveller must have felt when no one stopped to help him at first. Then the children can talk about ways in which they can help others in their daily lives.

Older children can make posters about ways they can help people. Encourage the children to be original. It is the creative children of today who can grow up to have creative solutions to world problems tomorrow. We must encourage the children to think and to use their imaginations.

In her book *How to Be a Very, Very, Very, Very Good Catechist,* Margaret Timmerman M.H.S.H. defines creativity. She says, "What is meant by creativity? It is described as the capacity in an individual to see new relationships and possibilities in familiar objects, ideas, and situations, and to produce something novel as a result."[3]

Each child needs to be encouraged to have a unique and creative outlook. We need to make use of their God-given gifts and talents. We must allow them the freedom to express their ideas and opinions. The posters can be made into a hall display that the other classes can study as they pass through the area.

Helping Hands

Remind the children that God calls us all to a life of love. Encourage them to think of ways that they can show love to others. Some of the ways children might express love for others are:

> Sharing a toy
> Giving a hug to grandparents
> Drawing a picture for someone
> Telling parents that you love them
> Setting the table
> Showing a younger child how to play a game
> Putting away toys
> Helping someone look for a lost object
> Taking turns on the swings
> Playing with a new child

Encourage the children to think of ways in their own lives that they can be of service to others. Help them to realize that we all have the ability and the opportunity to help others.

---

[3]Margaret Timmerman, M.H.S.H., *How to Be a Very, Very, Very, Very Good Catechist* (Mystic, Conn.: Twenty-Third Publications, 1981), p. 64. Used by permission of Twenty-Third Publications.

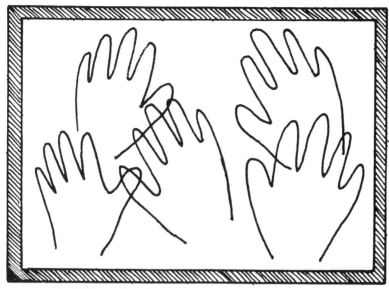

Figure 5-3. Helping Hands.

The children can make a drawing of their helping hands so they remember to help others. On a piece of white paper the children can draw around their hands with markers. Each hand shape should be a different color such as dark blue, green, purple, light blue, and red. This makes a pleasing collage effect. The bright outlines of the hand shapes stand out against the white paper. This art activity can be framed by gluing it to a coordinating color of construction paper (see illustration).

Donations

Children need to understand that care for others extends beyond their immediate family and friends into the world community. As members of the family of God, our responsibility is to all His people. We are to care about all the people of His flock.

To help the children learn about the needs of others, we can discuss with them various organizations that collect money for those in need. We can tell them about those who send food to people who are hungry, provide medical supplies for the ill, and provide shelter for those who have nowhere to go.

The class can vote on which organization they will collect money to aid. Set up a display area featuring pictures of the organization in action. Have a can in which donations can be placed. Encourage the children to earn the money by doing chores. Set a deadline for collecting money.

Encourage the children also to pray for all those in need and the people who help them. Pray for those who are ill, hurt, disabled, hungry, and homeless. Remember them in class prayers.

Service Projects

The only way to make caring a part of life is to practice it. It is this way with all learning tasks. We need to provide opportunities for children to practice what they learn. Only in this way will they be able to apply what they learn to their own lives.

Children learn to care for others by being personally involved. This involvement makes them aware of people who need our help in our communities. Children learn by doing. It is one thing to tell the children that Jesus wants us to love others. It is another to put the words into practice.

One way to help the children learn to care is with a service project. Several classes might get together and make tray favors for the residents of a nearby nursing home. This is more meaningful if the children go to the nursing home and personally deliver what they have made. Elderly people isolated in nursing homes love to see children. The personal contact lets these people know that someone cares.

It is important to check with the activity director of the nursing home as to what type of service project is needed and to follow the advice given. The time chosen to go on the field trip should also be decided in consultation with the activity director. Be sure to secure approval from the children's parents ahead of time.

Field trips such as this are great learning experiences for the children. They make the children aware of other people's needs. Field trips take the children outside the realm of their everyday lives. They expand the children's knowledge of what it means to be a member of God's family.

Service projects such as field trips must always be followed by discussion and evaluation if they are to be understood and meaningful to the children's lives. Ask the children what they liked and didn't like about the visit. Ask them how they think it feels to be old. See if they feel a sense of responsibility toward the elderly of our society.

Have them decide if they would like to go again. If so let them decide if they would do anything differently this time. Planning for a follow-up visit helps them to see that caring about people is a continuing process. It is not something done only once.

Role Playing

Role playing is an excellent activity that helps children put themselves in the place of others. It allows children to become aware of the needs and feelings of others. Children often have difficulty seeing beyond themselves. Role playing enables the children to practice making decisions. It allows them to consider alternative forms of behavior. They gain experience in dealing with various situations.

Since children learn best by doing, role playing affords them the opportunity to put into practice concepts and ideas that they have been studying in the classroom. It helps them translate abstract concepts such as caring into concrete terms and situations. Role playing allows the children to test out their ideas.

Role play situations that are presented should always be relevant to the children's lives. Ask for volunteers and choose specific children for each role. Then give the children some idea of the feelings of the various characters involved. Explain some of the conflicts inherent in the situation to be portrayed.

Let the audience know that they are an important part of the role play situation. Explain some things for which they should be looking. Let them know that they will have the chance to tell their ideas also.

The children involved in the role play situation should be the ones to decide what they will say and how they will act. The basic situation should be explained to the class and the children take it from there.

After each role play the characters involved should be asked how they felt in their roles. What made them decide to act as they did in that situation? Then all the children in the class can talk about whether or not the solution to the situation presented was a fair one.

The children should switch roles so that they can get an idea of how all the people feel in a given situation. Eventually all children who want to participate should be allowed to do so. There may be many workable solutions to each problem situation.

After each role play session, the teacher should help the children draw some general conclusions and observations about behavior toward others. This will help the children apply what they have learned to other situations they may encounter.

Some situations that can be role played by children include the following:

> You are riding your bicycle to school with several of your friends. It is almost time for the bell to ring. One child hits the curb with his bike and falls off. He doesn't get hurt, but his lunchbox and papers are scattered. The other children have ridden on ahead so they won't be late.
>
> You are swinging at recess. You and a friend are seeing who can go the highest. As you look down, you see a new child sitting on the bench alone.
>
> You see your brother playing with matches. He says that if you tell your mom that he will tell her that you broke a neighbor child's toy last week on purpose.
>
> You are waiting in line at the drinking fountain. Suddenly someone pushes you trying to get a drink without going to the back of the line. He knocks you into another child who starts to cry.
>
> A new family is moving in next door. You see toys being unloaded that indicate that there must be a child about your age in the family. Your friend comes over and you decide to go over and meet the new child. Just then the door to the new neighbor's house opens. A child comes slowly out on the front porch. You see that she wears leg braces and uses crutches.

One result of role playing is that the children often discover that it isn't always easy to do the right thing. However, the more experience that they have in dealing with various situations, the better they are able to decide on the best course of action.

Speakers

Children learn by example. It is one thing for us to tell the children that they should care about others. It is a greater lesson if they see how those words can be put into action in various ways. Invite speakers to come in and talk to the class about different ways that they have found to serve others as a vocation or an avocation.

Speakers can make children more aware of ways that people can help people. Speakers can encourage the children to see Christianity as a way of life and not just something talked about in the classroom.

Usually there are people right in our own churches who can come in and talk to the children and answer their questions. These speakers can tell the children about what they have chosen to do, why they chose to do what they do, and why they feel that it is important.

Speakers who represent a Christian way of life include the following:

Doctors, nurses, paramedics
Teachers of handicapped children
Physical therapists who help stroke victims
Pastors
Foster parents
Peace Corp volunteers
People who deliver "Meals on Wheels"
Hospital volunteers

Saints

We all need heroes to admire and respect. As teachers in religious education, we need to provide children with Christian heroes. The lives of some of the saints are fascinating accounts of the ways in which various people throughout the ages have followed God's will.

St. Francis, for example, is one saint who is universally admired even 800 years later. We celebrate his feast day on October 4. We can tell the children about his life.

Francis Bernadone lived in the town of Assisi in Italy in the late 1100s and early 1200s. He was the son of a wealthy merchant. When he was 20 years old he became a soldier, was captured, and spent a year in prison.

When he was released, Francis had changed. He felt that God was calling him. He gave away everything he owned. This made his father very angry.

Francis went around the countryside telling people about God's love for all of us. He began calling himself Brother Francis to emphasize that we are all brothers and sisters in Christ.

Statues of St. Francis often show him with a bird perched on his shoulder. This is because Francis loved all God's creatures. Many stories are told about Francis talking to the animals and how they listened to him. One story is about a mean wolf who was terrorizing the town of Gubbio. Francis went out in the woods and talked to the wolf. He told him to leave the people of the town alone and he did.

Francis wanted all people to love God. To help them understand the true meaning of Christmas, he made the first nativity scene using local people and animals to represent the first Christmas.

Francis attracted followers who wanted to live simply as he did and spread the Gospel to all people. Today his followers are called Franciscans and they follow the rules that St. Francis set down for them. Indeed

St. Francis is a Christian hero. His life exemplified love of God and neighbor.

Role Models

There are many people in our own day and age who have adopted Christianity as a way of life. They provide role models for us. They show us that one person can make a difference.

One such person is Mother Teresa. We can tell the children about Mother Teresa's work among the poorest of the poor in India. She and her followers, called the Missionaries of Charity, care for poor people who are dying in Calcutta. Mother Teresa has also founded houses providing care in other areas. Mother Teresa and her sisters let these people know that someone cares about them. They feed and nurse these people who have nowhere to go to die. Thousands of people have been cared for by them.

We need to point out to the children that we all make choices. Some things happen to us by chance or circumstances, but it is what we do with our talents and abilities that is important.

Encourage the children to bring in newspaper clippings about people who care for others. Read these stories to the children. Stories such as those about families who adopt handicapped children are good for such a project.

Allow the children to discuss why these people do what they do. Then the stories can be posted on a bulletin board marked "People Who Care." Then those children who want to review the stories on their own can do so. This idea is one that can help children learn about love and caring about others. They can learn about other people who have followed Jesus' command that we love one another.

chapter 6

Praising God Through Prayer and Music

We talk to God and He talks to us through prayer. Prayer is an expression of our faith and trust in God. Prayer is our way of sharing our feelings with God. Through prayer we praise God for His glory, we say we are sorry for the times we have not done His will, we ask His help in all that we do, and we thank God for His gifts to us.

In order to help children learn to pray, we as teachers need to make prayer a part of our lives. We need to pray that we will be effective teachers of His children. We need to remember always for Whom we teach.

Children learn by doing. They will learn to pray by praying. A class should be a faith community that prays together.

Music is praying also. It is said that when we sing, we pray twice. Music is a God-given gift to us. Music can be a wonderful way for children to express love and praise to God. Music can be their way of communicating their feelings with God. It can help children tell God what they cannot express in words.

In their book *Celebrating Jesus,* Rev. Carey Landry and Carol Jean Kinghorn express the importance of music:

> Sharing our Faith is a joyful, freeing experience. God has provided us with a unique method of sharing—music. Music can touch the heart. It can uncover and reveal to us what is deepest in our hearts allowing our thoughts and feelings to be known to us. Music has the power to take words beyond their limit and say what can be said in no other way.[1]

[1] The above quote is an excerpt from the book *Celebrating Jesus* by Rev. Carey Landry and Carol Jean Kinghorn, pg 7. Copyright © 1977 by North American Liturgy Resources, 10802 North 23rd Avenue, Phoenix, Arizona 85029. All rights reserved. Used with permission.

Whenever children come together to learn about God, there should be prayer and music. Both are a natural part of celebrating God's love and His many gifts to us. Various ways to help children learn to praise God through prayer and music follow.

Talking

Discuss prayer with the children. Ask them how they tell things to their families and friends. They will probably mention ways that include talking and listening. We can explain to them that prayer is our way of talking with God and listening to Him. We also pray through all that we do.

Let the children name places where they pray. They will think of such places as church, class, and home. Remind them that we can pray anywhere. God is with us everywhere we go.

Ask the children to name times when they pray. They may name bedtime and mealtime. Tell them that we can pray anytime. We can pray when we are happy or sad or lonely or afraid. God is always waiting. He is always watching over us.

Prayer Pictures

Children too young to read can use prayer pictures as a beginning prayer experience.

Cut pictures out of magazines such as animals, flowers, people, and other things that God has made. Spread the pictures out on a table and allow each child to pick a picture. Then the children can gather in a circle for prayer.

Each child in turn can name what is in the picture and say thank you to God for it. For example, if Nancy chose a picture of a tulip, she might say "Thank you, God, for red flowers." If Jon chose a picture of a family, he could say "Thank you, God, for families who love us." The prayer should be the child's own.

Thank You Shapes

Children enjoy cutting shapes out of construction paper. Let them cut out things for which they are thankful. Shapes can be precut for young children. Some shapes that can be used are a sun, a leaf, a person, a squirrel, or a bird (see illustration).

Figure 6-1. Thank You Shape.

Then the children can write prayers on their shapes. Young children can dictate their prayers to their teachers to write. Prayers should be simple such as "Thank you, God, for people who help us" or "Thank you, God, for brown, furry squirrels." Then the children can sign their names.

The children can punch a hole in the top of each shape with a hole punch. Then the children can thread a length of yarn through the hole. Teachers can hang the prayer shapes from the ceiling as reminders of gifts for which we can thank God. Each time the children enter the room, they will be reminded of the many gifts that God has given us. These shapes will be a visible sign of God's presence through the things that He made for us. This idea is from *Living in God's Love* by Jeanne Coolahan Mueller.[2]

Letters to God

Discuss with the class what types of letters people usually write to friends or relatives. Sometimes letters tell what has been happening in

[2]Jeanne Coolahan Mueller, *Living in God's Love,* Vacation Bible School Series Planning Guide (Minneapolis, Minn.: Augsburg Publishing House, 1981), p. 29. Used by permission of Augsburg Publishing House.

people's lives. Letters also can be a way of telling others how the writers feel about people, places, and events. Other times letters are a request for help or a thank you for past kindnesses.

Ask the children to write letters to God. Explain to them that the letters will not be mailed, but that God will see them as He sees all that we do.

This activity helps the children to see God as someone with whom they can share their thoughts and feelings. God cares about even the most mundane happenings if they are important to the children. The children can tell God about anything and everything.

Tell the children not to sign their letters. Let them know that the letters will be shared with their classmates. Collect the letters when the children are finished writing. The next time that the class meets, read the letters to the class.

Through writing letters to God, the children have the experience of sharing what is in their hearts. Knowing that the other children have similar thoughts and worries makes it easier to pray.

Cinquain Poems

Older children will enjoy making up their own prayers using the cinquain poetry form. This format can be used for lovely prayers. The students may be surprised at their ability and be proud of their accomplishment using this poetry form. Explain the cinquain to them. The directions can be written on the board or on a poster that all the children can see:

> Line 1: A title (1 word)
> Line 2: Descriptive words (2 words)
> Line 3: Action words (3 words)
> Line 4: Feeling about the title (4 words)
> Line 5: Synonym of the title (1 word)

Teachers can suggest the theme or title. All the children can work together to write a prayer. As the students suggest the words, they can be written on the blackboard. Then the class can say the prayer together. Such a prayer can be the following:

> Jesus
> loved others
> caring, calling, comforting
> friend who loves me
> Savior

The students may also write their own individual prayers following this poetry form. Good themes are life, love, and caring. This idea is from *Living in God's Love* by Jeanne Coolahan Mueller.[3]

Psalms

The psalms can be used for beautiful prayers. Children might take turns each week reading a psalm at the beginning of class. Another way to use psalms is to say the first line of each two and have the children say the refrain. A good psalm that can be used is Psalm 136. Verses 1-9 and 25-26 follow:

> Give thanks to Yahweh, for he is good,
> his love is everlasting!
> Give thanks to the God of gods,
> his love is everlasting!
> Give thanks to the Lord of lords,
> his love is everlasting!
>
> He alone performs great marvels,
> his love is everlasting!
> His wisdom made the heavens,
> his love is everlasting!
> He set the earth on the waters,
> his love is everlasting!
>
> He made the great lights,
> his love is everlasting!
> The sun to govern the day,
> his love is everlasting!
> Moon and starts to govern the night,
> his love is everlasting . . .
>
> He provides for all living creatures,
> his love is everlasting!
> Give thanks to the God of Heaven,
> his love is everlasting!

Afterward the children can draw or paint pictures of what the psalm represents to them. The mental images that were invoked by the reading of the psalm can be put down on paper as a way of extending the prayer experience.

The psalms can also be read as slides are projected on a screen. This makes a meaningful meditation. A church member might be able to provide suitable slides. It is also possible to purchase slides and filmstrips with recordings or narrations that can be used as prayers. This

[3]Mueller, p. 22.

provides a variety of prayer experiences that can expand our concept of God.

Formal Prayer

Children also need to memorize formal prayers. Formal prayers allow us to pray together as a community. They remind us of truths.

Prayer time can be made special for the children with the use of signs and symbols. Children can join hands as they pray. The power of touch is amazing. It forms a bond between people. Candles can be lit for prayer time. Flickering flames fascinate children. We can use candles to explain to children that Jesus is the light of our lives and we are to follow Him. This is why candles are used in church and one reason why the advent wreath is so popular at Christmas.

Prayer should always end with a moment of silence. Silence allows children to ponder the meaning of the prayer they have just said. It allows them to add their own personal message to God. Also it allows them to feel God's presence all around them. Silence offers an opportunity to let God speak to each of them.

Gestures

Children like to use gestures with prayers such as the Lord's Prayer. Gestures help the children learn and understand the prayer they are saying. Gestures allow the children to move around and express their feelings to God through actions as well as words. Gestures promote a real feeling of involvement in prayer because the children use their bodies as well as their voices to praise God.

Some gestures that can be used to accompany the Lord's Prayer are the following:

Our Father, who art in heaven,	(Arms raised above head)
hallowed be Thy name.	(Arms crossed across chest)
Thy kingdom come; Thy will be done on earth as it is in heaven.	(Hands extended forward)
Give us this day our daily bread;	(Arms extended at sides)
And forgive us our trespasses as we forgive those who trespass against us;	(Hands crossed over heart)

And lead us not into temptation,   (Hands folded as in prayer)
but deliver us from evil.

Amen   (Arms raised above head)

Prayer Banners

Children do need reminders to pray. One way to help them remember to pray is through making individual prayer banners. These can be hung on the doorknobs to the children's rooms at home. Each time they see the banners, they will be reminded to pray.

To make prayer banners, cut heavy paper into pieces about ten inches long and five inches wide. Cut a round hole near the top of each banner so that it can be slipped over a doorknob.

Each banner should bear a symbol of Jesus that will remind the children of Him and thus of prayer. The fish is a good symbol as is a heart.

Prayer banners will encourage the children to pray. The banners will help the children remember Jesus' presence in their lives.

Prayerful Actions

It is important to stress to the children that prayer is not just for bedtime or for church. Prayer isn't just words, it is actions also.

Every time we admire a sunset, we are praying. Every time we stop to say hello to a lonely neighbor, we are praying. Every time we help someone, we are praying.

We pray through everything that we do. In trying always to do our best and to do God's will, we are praying. Prayer is a way of life. It is staying in touch with God. It is seeking Him. It is loving Him above all else.

Prayer Wheel

A prayer wheel can help young children become aware of the various things for which they might pray. This project helps put the abstract concept of prayer into an understandable form for children.

Talk to the children about things for which they might pray. Encourage them to think of things for which they might thank God such as food, people, animals, sunshine, leaves, and flowers. Let them think of their own ideas.

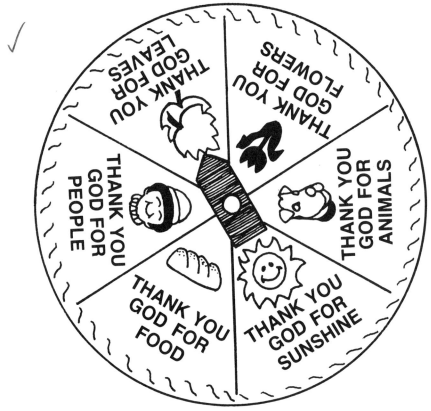

Figure 6-2. Prayer Wheel.

Give each child a large paper plate to make a prayer wheel. Help them divide the plate into six equal pie-shaped pieces. Use a ruler and pen to mark the areas. In each section the children can place a picture of something for which they might pray. Pictures can be cut from magazines and glued onto the paper plate.

The name of each item chosen can be printed underneath the picture with the words "Thank you God for . . . ." Then attach a paper pointer to the middle of the plate with a brad (see illustration). The pointer can be cut from construction paper.

Encourage the children to use their prayer wheels at home for prayer. They can turn the pointer to the picture they want. Then they can offer a prayer of thanksgiving for that part of God's creation. The prayer wheel is a great help to children just learning to pray. It helps remind them of the many gifts for which we can give thanks to God. This idea is adapted from *God's People Together in Christ* by Sharon Dale.[4]

Prayer Cards

Explain to the children that we ask God's help in all that we do because without Him we can do nothing. Let them know that as brothers and sisters in Christ we should pray for the needs of all God's people. Help the children to think of some people who might need our prayers. Then encourage each child to write a petition on an index card. Petitions can include phrases such as the following:

> We pray for those who are ill
> Remember people who live in war-torn lands.
> Guide those who are in prisons.
> Help government leaders to make wise decisions.
> Comfort those who are dying.
> Remember children who go to bed hungry at night.
> Help people who are lonely.
> We pray for those children caught in unhappy home situations.
> Bless those who teach us.

As the children finish writing their petitions they should join the teacher in a prayer circle on the floor. The teacher should have a petition also. The teacher can begin the prayer and the children can take turns reading their prayers. The prayer can be ended by the teacher with a general prayer asking for God's blessing on all of His people.

After the "Amen" the children can post their prayer cards on the bulletin board under a heading such as "Lord God, hear our prayers." This will serve as a reminder to the children to pray for others. It will encourage them to ask God's help for others as well as for themselves.

Prayer Chart

A way to encourage children to learn memorized prayers is to use a class prayer chart. On a piece of posterboard print all the children's names in a column on the left-hand side. Across the top print the name of each prayer the children should know. Fill in the chart with intersect-

---

[4]"Prayer Wheel" adapted by permission from 1981 Vacation Bible School Series Planning Guide, *God's People Together in Christ,* copyright 1980 Augsburg Publishing House, page 28. Used by permission of Augsburg Publishing House.

ing lines so that next to each child's name is a square corresponding to each prayer.

It is helpful to the children and their parents to send home copies of the prayers that the children are to learn. The children enjoy it most if the prayers are made into individual booklets.

Each time a child learns a prayer by heart, put a star in the appropriate square. Each prayer should have a different color star. Keep the chart where everyone can see it as a way to promote competition and encourage the children.

Music

Music seems to have a universal appeal to all kinds of children. Many wonderful songs are written now just for children. Simple lyrics and joyful melodies speak the language of children.

Records can be playing as the children come into class. They can listen to records while they work on art activities and other class projects.

Children can quickly learn to sing along with records. Many of the good children's records have accompanying song books that suggest gestures and movements that the children can use to accompany the songs.

Gestures are important for children. They allow the children to express themselves. Appropriate gestures carry out the theme and meaning of a song. They allow the children to sing and pray in a way that is meaningful to them. They enrich the children's understanding. Gestures allow a child to express a personal relationship with God.

Instruments

Children like to create their own music with instruments. In the religious education classroom we can provide opportunities for the children to explore various types of instruments such as cymbals, tambourines, triangles, shakers, drums, and rhythm sticks.

The children enjoy having a praise parade where they march around the room in time to music and play their instruments. This is a joyful way to celebrate God's love.

Songs

Singing is a natural way for children to praise God. Children love to sing. It helps them learn about God and themselves. Singing also builds community since the children share a common experience.

Familiar melodies can sometimes be used as the basis for creative songs for children in religious education classes. These tunes are easy for the children to learn if they do not already know them. They can be sung alone or with piano or guitar accompaniment.

In her article "Summer Celebrations" in *Religion Teacher's Journal,* Ginny Janas gives ideas for three songs that can be sung to familiar tunes.[5]

A good creation song for young children is "God Our Father Made a World." This is sung to the tune of "Old MacDonald Had a Farm." The children can take turns inserting the name of an animal and its sounds at appropriate places in the song.

Another song is sung to the tune of "Frere Jacques":

I Am Special

I am special. I am special.
If you look, you will see
someone very special,
someone very special,
Yes, it's me. Yes, it's me.

She also suggests the following song with gestures which is sung to the tune of "Twinkle, Twinkle, Little Star":

God Made You and God Made Me

God made the earth (describe a small ball),
And God made the sky (large circle over head),
God made the fish (waving movements with hands),
And the birds that fly (flap arms at sides).
Animals (touch floor with hands),
Flowers (Pick up and smell flowers),
Trees so tall (stand up and stretch):
God made everything
Great (extend arms) and small (bring hands together).
God made all (arms outstretched)

[5]Ginny Janas, "Summer Celebrations," *Religion Teacher's Journal,* 14.4 (May/June 1980), pgs. 17, 18, 21. Used by permission.

That I can see (shield eyes with hands, look side to side).
God made you (point to others)
And God made me (point to self)

Music is an important experience for children. It allows them to express their love of God, our Father. Music allows children to delight in being His children.

chapter 7

Exploring the Bible

It is important for children to learn about the Bible. The values of the Gospels are those that they are expected to live as Christians. Knowing the Bible helps us live the message of Jesus more fully. The Bible helps children understand what God wants of His people.

The Bible tells the story of God's unfailing love for His people. It is important that children understand their heritage as people of God. The Bible also provides examples of people who have sought God even when it wasn't easy to do.

Children should be introduced to the Bible as a collection of stories about God's love. Children like stories and enjoy listening to them. Children are curious and eager to learn. As teachers we can encourage this enthusiasm for learning by using Bible stories as part of the lesson.

We must be certain to always explain Bible times and customs to the children. The Bible was written by people in another time and place. Terms such as "shepherd," "leper," and "Samaritan" must be carefully explained to the children if they are to understand the story. To a young child a shepherd is a large dog, not someone who tends sheep. Bible terms can confuse children if they do not understand what is being said.

The Bible story must always be chosen to carry out and reinforce the theme of the lesson. This leads to greater understanding and comprehension. The story also should be related to the children's own experiences. This is how they learn and remember. They must be able to see how they can use the message of the Bible story in their own lives. With the teacher's guidance, the children can explore ways to implement the Bible lesson in their lives now and in the future.

Hopefully, as the children grow so will their understanding and appreciation of the Bible. They should be introduced to Bible stories that they can understand. The joy that the children find in hearing Bible stories and in various Bible activities will provide an incentive to seek the Bible later in their lives also.

Following are some activities that can be used to help children explore the Bible.

Reading Bible Stories

Children learn only from Bible stories that they can understand and relate in some way to their own lives. The story of creation (Genesis 1:1-31, 2:1-3) is one of the best Bible stories for young children. They can relate the story to what they see around them in nature. It is within the realm of their experience.

The New Testament, especially the Gospels, is a good source of Bible stories for children. Some of these are the following:

Good Samaritan	Luke 10:30-37
Jesus and the Children	Mark 10:13-16
Good Shepherd	John 10:11-15
Jesus and the Fishermen	Luke 5:1-11
Loaves and Fishes	Mark 6:30-44
Cure of the Blind Man	Mark 10:46-52
Prodigal Son	Luke 15:11-32
Ten Lepers	Luke 17:11-19
Cure of the Lame Man	Luke 5:17-26
Zacchaeus	Luke 19:1-10

It is best to read a simplified version of the story. A children's Bible or Bible storybook can be used successfully because they are written with children in mind. They are easier for children to understand and follow.

After reading a Bible story to the children, follow with questions that will ascertain their understanding of the story. Help them relate the Bible stories to their own lives.

Bible tapes are available that can be used by individual children as a review of a Bible story. Bible story tapes can also be made by reading a story into a tape recorder. These should be accompanied by a copy of a Bible storybook so that the children can look at the pictures as they listen to the story.

Storytelling

Throughout the ages people have communicated through stories. Bible stories were told from person to person before they were ever written down. Telling Bible stories to children is an excellent means of communicating Jesus' message.

Telling Bible stories allows the teacher to interact directly with the children and tailor the story to suit the interest of the children. The storyteller can look directly at the children as the story is told and help them feel that the story is being told directly to them. Appropriate gestures can be used to emphasize dramatic moments in the story.

Storytelling allows the teachers to paint a visual picture that encourages the children to use their imaginations. Telling stories weaves a magic spell around the children that takes them beyond the classroom and into the time of Jesus.

Storytelling is an art. In order to tell Bible stories, it is necessary to know the story well. The storyteller must have a visual image of the characters in the story in order to effectively present them to the children. Also, the storyteller must be able to use voice inflections effectively to hold the attention of the children.

It is necessary to capture the attention of the children before beginning the story. Introduce the children to the story in a way that gives them a reason to listen. Establish a personal link between the story and the children.

Stories have a universal appeal for children. Sometimes they can help children learn in a way that no other teaching method can do. It is a good method for helping children explore Bible stories.

Echo Pantomimes

Echo pantomimes are a great way to help children learn Bible stories. Children learn best by being actively involved in the lesson. Through echo pantomimes the children and teachers tell the story together.

The teacher says a line of the story and performs the accompanying action. Then the students immediately repeat the line and the action. This is continued throughout the story. The children will remember the story told this way longer because they did it rather than just heard it. Activities such as this one make learning fun.

Zacchaeus (Based on Luke 19:1-10)

Jesus went to the city of Jericho.	(walk in place)
There was a rich tax collector named Zacchaeus.	(collect money)
He was very short.	(stoop down)
He wanted to see who Jesus was,	(stand up, shade eyes)
but couldn't see over the crowd.	(stand on tiptoes, look around)
So Zacchaeus ran to a sycamore tree.	(run in place)
He climbed the tree.	(tree-climbing motions)
When Jesus came walking by,	(walk in place)
he looked up.	(shade eyes, look up)
"Hurry down, Zacchaeus," he said,	(arm motion to come)
"because I will stay at your house today."	(point yonder)
Zacchaeus hurried down	(climbing motions)
to welcome Jesus to his house.	(outstretched arms)
The crowd grumbled,	(angry look, hands on waist)
"This man has gone home with a sinner."	(whisper to neighbor)
And at Zacchaeus' house—	(point yonder)
Jesus and Zacchaeus ate together	(eating motions)
Zacchaeus said to Jesus,	(motion as if standing)
"I will give half of what I have to the poor;	(pointing to self)
and if I have cheated anyone,	(put money in pocket)
I will pay him back four times as much."	(hold up four fingers)
Jesus said to Zacchaeus,	(point ahead)
"Salvation has come to this house today."	(hands outstretched)

These ideas are adapted from the article "Echo Pantomimes Intrigue Teachers and Learners" in *Church Teachers Magazine* by Joan Lilja.[1]

Panorama

A Bible story panorama involves all the children in the class. Several large sheets of paper are provided so that the children can draw parts of a Bible story. Two or three children can be assigned various scenes to draw together on their sheet of paper.

Children enjoy art activities such as this. It also helps them to understand the story. The scenes can be hung on a hallway wall in the order of the story. Thus, other children will also learn from this project as they look at the pictures. Each picture should be labeled with the words to the part of the story that it represents.

[1]Joan Lilja, "Echo Pantomimes Intrigue Teachers and Learners," *Church Teachers Magazine,* 10 No. 4 (March/April/May 1983), p. 186. Used by permission of *Church Teachers Magazine* published by the National Teacher Education Program.

The children can do panoramas such as the following:

The Big Catch of Fish (based on Luke 5:1-11)

First panel	One day Jesus went out in Peter's boat.
Second panel	Jesus told Peter to put out the fishing nets.
Third panel	The fishermen caught so many fish that the nets were full.
Fourth panel	Another boat had to come and help them.
Fifth panel	Jesus told Peter that He would make him a fisher of men.

Figure 7-1. Rhyme Puzzle.

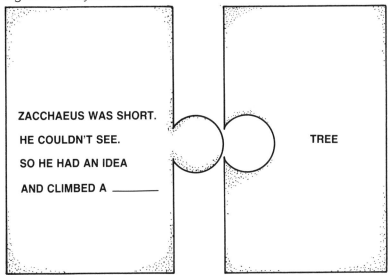

Rhyme Puzzles

Children enjoy being able to demonstrate their knowledge of Bible stories with rhyme puzzles. Two piece puzzles can be cut out of file folders for the children to put together. On one piece is written a Bible rhyme with the rhyming word missing. On the matching piece is written the missing word (see illustration). The children match up the puzzle pieces and put them together.

This activity helps the children recall Bible stories that they have been learning. Children like rhymes and puzzles and the two together are a fun learning activity. The children know right away if they have found the correct word to complete the rhyme. If the puzzle pieces interlock, the answer is right.

Bible rhymes such as the following can be used:

Zaccheus was short.
He couldn't see.
So he had an idea
and climbed a _____.   tree

Jesus gave Peter
a command to keep:
Feed my lambs,
feed my _____.   sheep

The little children
wanted to see.
So Jesus said:
bring them to _____.   Me

The blind Bartimaeus
knew it was right.
To ask the Lord Jesus
to restore his _____.   sight

From all over Galilee
the people came.
They saw Jesus cure
the blind and the _____.   lame

Round Robin

To help children review Bible stories that they have studied in previous years, the round robin method of storytelling can be used.

The children sit in a circle. The teacher starts out the story. For example, to retell the story of Jesus' cure of the lame man, the teacher can say, "Once upon a time there was a man who couldn't walk." Each child adds a sentence to the story as the turn passes to the right around the circle. This continues until the story has been told. The children may get more than one turn depending upon how lengthly the story becomes.

This is a great activity because it involves the children in telling the story. It helps them review a story without having it read to them. Also there are no wrong answers because the story can be embellished in the retelling. This activity also helps the children learn from one another.

The teacher can also tape record the story as the children tell it. Then the tape can be played for the class. This provides an additional review of the story. The children will enjoy hearing how they sound.

Bible Book

Each child in the class can make a children's Bible book. Each time the children hear a Bible story in class, they can draw a picture of their favorite part of the story for their Bible books.

A book can be made by fastening two pieces of construction paper together with brads to make a book cover. On the cover the children can put "My Book of Bible Stories by . . ." and their name. The teacher can print the title for younger children.

The inside pages of the book can be inexpensive sheets of typing paper. Each page should be labeled with the title of the Bible story studied. The teacher can provide paper with the titles already printed on for younger children. On these pages the children draw their Bible pictures each time the class has a Bible story.

Drawing helps aid retention. The children will remember the stories over a longer period of time if they have illustrated each one. Since Bible stories are full of action, an appropriate picture is not difficult to draw. The children will be proud to take their books home. In future weeks they might also look at their book and it will provide a meaningful way to remember Bible stories.

Fishing for Bible Verses

This is an enjoyable activity for the children. Fishing for Bible verses helps the children become familiar with a variety of verses from the Bible.

Cut out brightly colored paper fish. Attach a paper clip to the nose of each fish. Younger children can fish for fish with Bible verses printed on them. The teachers can read the Bible verses to the children as they catch the fish.

Fishing poles are made from wooden dowels. Tie a piece of string onto the end of the pole. On the other end of the string tie a magnet (see illustration). The magnets will attract the metal paper clips and the children will be able to catch fish.

Older children can catch fish with Bible references on one side. The children can later look up the reference themselves and print it on the other side of the fish. To make the game more interesting, there can be a rule that the children must catch one fish of each color. If they catch a second fish of the same color, they must throw it back in the pond on the floor.

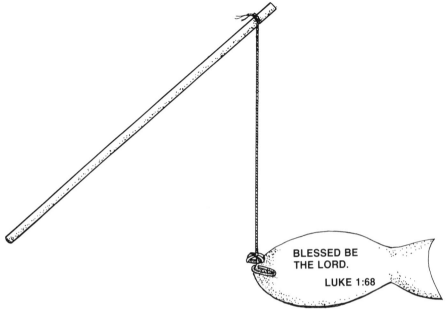

Figure 7-2. Fishing for Bible Verses.

This is a fun way to help children learn about Bible verses. The children can take home all their fish to keep. Good Bible verses that can be used include the following:

As the Father has loved me, so I have loved you . . .	John 15:9
Blessed be the Lord . . .	Luke 1:68
What I command you is to love one another.	John 15:17
Ask and it will be given to you . . .	Matthew 7:7
Jesus said, "You must love the Lord your God with all your heart . . ."	Matthew 22:37
Glory to God in the highest . . .	Luke 2:14
By this love you have for one another, everyone will know that you are my disciples.	John 13:35
Acclaim God all the earth . . .	Psalm 66:1

Bible Placemats

Children learn by doing. Craft projects such as Bible placemats help them to learn and remember. Craft projects involve students in the learning process and make learning fun.

The craft project that the children do should always carry out the theme of the day's lesson. Bible placemats can be used to help the children remember the day's Bible story.

Each child should pick out a sheet of colored construction paper. On these sheets the children print and illustrate a Bible verse. Younger children will need to have the Bible verse printed for them. They can draw a picture or cut shapes out of other colors of construction paper and glue them onto their placemats. If they are working on the Bible verse "I am the Good Shepherd . . ." (John 10:14), the children could make sheep on their placemats (see illustration).

As a finishing touch the children should fringe all the edges with scissors. Half-inch deep cuts make an attractive fringe. Since craft projects such as this are fairly structured, the children's ability to complete them often depends on their physical development. Teachers should quietly help the children who cannot cut well with scissors. Teachers should also praise the children's efforts and show confidence in their ability.

The children can take home their placemats to use at mealtime. To make the placemats last longer, they can be covered with clear adhesive paper. The children will be proud to take home their placemats and show their parents. Craft projects that are taken home such as this one provide a basis for discussion with parents. The parents

Figure 7-3. Bible Placemat.

I AM THE GOOD SHEPHERD

are then aware of what the children are studying. The idea for Bible placemats comes from *The Big Book of Bible Crafts and Projects* by Joy Mackenzie.[2]

Bible Puzzles

Young children enjoy putting together puzzles. This provides a great sense of accomplishment when a child successfully completes a puzzle. Puzzles are good activities for early arrivals to the classroom.

Bible puzzles can be made from pictures from children's Bible books. Use a glue stick to attach the puzzle to cardboard. Cover with clear self-adhesive paper. Cut the picture into 12 pieces like a jigsaw puzzle. Store each puzzle in a small box with a duplicate picture glued to the top. This provides a guide for the children to follow.

Sponge Painting

Sponge painting is a fun Bible art activity for children. It helps them remember the Bible story that they have heard. Arts and crafts are important learning tools for children. They help children express themselves. They aid understanding.

In sponge painting, sponges are cut into various shapes with scissors. The shape should be representative of the story that the children are studying. Fish shapes can be used for the story of Jesus and the fishermen. Flower shapes can be used for the story of creation.

Bright colors of tempra paint work well with this project. Several different colors should be available for the children. Each sponge shape is used for one color of paint, thus several sponge shapes are needed for each project.

To make sponge paintings, the children dip a shape into the paint and stamp the design on their papers. Manilla construction paper works well and provides a neutral background. The children should be encouraged to use several colors on their paintings.

Spring-type clothespins can be used for handles for the sponges. This keeps fingers out of paint. Paint shirts should be worn since children sometimes lean on their papers.

---

[2] Joy Mackenzie, *The Big Book of Bible Crafts and Projects* (Nashville, TN: Impact Books, 1981, reassigned to The Zondervan Corporation, Grand Rapids, MI, 1982), p. 171. Used by permission of The Zondervan Corporation.

Title each child's sponge painting with the Bible story that it represents. Thus, the children will be reminded of the Bible story each time they look at their paintings at home.

Flannelboard Stories

Using a flannelboard to tell Bible stories is a favorite with teachers and children. Young children especially enjoy seeing Bible stories brought alive with flannelboard figures. Visual aids are very important in working with children. Flannelboards make stories interesting. They help children to visualize the story.

The teacher should be familiar enough with the Bible story to tell it rather than read it. As the various characters are mentioned in the story, the teacher places the Bible figures on the flannelboard. The flannelboard can be placed on the floor and the children seated in front of it. This way everyone will have a good view.

Flannelboards are very effective with such Bible stories as creation and the birth of Jesus. Children also enjoy helping to retell familiar Bible stories. Each child can be responsible for placing a figure on the flannelboard at the appropriate time in the story.

Filmstrips

Filmstrips can be an effective teaching tool for children. They provide an alternative way to present Bible stories to children. Bright, colorful pictures easily hold the interest of the children. The sequence of pictures that a filmstrip provides can increase understanding of a Bible story.

Teachers should always preview filmstrips to be sure that they are suitable for the age level of the children in the class. This also allows the opportunity to be sure that the filmstrip and accompanying cassette or record are in top condition.

It is important to introduce the filmstrip and let the children know what they can expect to see. Relate the story to a similar one that they have heard. Tell the children something that they should watch for especially. This stimulates their interest and helps hold their attention. If the filmstrip has a cassette tape, it can be stopped at appropriate points to allow questions or discussion.

After the filmstrip ask follow-up questions to be sure that the children understood the story. Sometimes filmstrips come with guides that have a list of appropriate questions. Allow time for discussion. Give the children a chance to reflect on what they have seen. Help them to sort out their ideas and impressions. Do not rush right into the next activity. Allow time for learning.

Bible Verse Tree

A Bible verse tree is a way to help children learn a Bible verse. The children paste a brown tree trunk on a sheet of blue construction paper. The tree should have bare branches.

   The children print the Bible verse in several parts on green tree sections cut from construction paper. All the children can learn one Bible verse or they can each pick one for their tree. The tree sections

Figure 7-4. Bible Verse Tree.

should be precut and printed ahead of time for younger children. The Bible reference is printed on the tree trunk.

For example, the reference John 13:35 can be put on the tree trunk. One tree section would say "By this love you have." The second section would say "for one another." The third section would be "everyone will know." The final section would read "that you are my disciples."

The children can practice saying the Bible verse and putting the tree sections in the correct order on the tree. When they feel that they have learned it, they can glue the tree in place. Then they can take their tree home and use it to remind themselves of the Bible verse (see illustration). This tree idea comes from *The Big Book of Bible Crafts and Projects* by Joy Mackenzie.[3]

Bible Times Newspaper

Older children who can read and write can have fun with a Bible newspaper. Each child can be assigned a Bible person, place, or custom about which to write a short story. Easy to read reference books should be available to the children to do the research.

When the children have had adequate time to research and write about their assigned topic, they should turn in their stories. A few sentences are enough. Each story should have a short title and be signed with the writer's name.

The stories can be assembled by the teacher into a one-page newspaper called "The Bible Times." Each story should bear the story title and writer's name. The stories should be written as if they happened today. The newspapers can be one page long and thus easy to duplicate for each child. They can also be given to other classes as a source of information.

Bible Places

It is very helpful for older students to study Bible places. This enables them to visualize more clearly the Bible stories that they hear about Jesus travelling from place to place. The study of Bible places helps the children to tie together the stories of the Gospels.

[3]Joy Mackenzie, *The Big Book of Bible Crafts and Projects* (Nashville, TN: Impact Books, 1981, reassigned to The Zondervan Corporation, Grand Rapids, MI, 1982), p. 168. Used by permission of The Zondervan Corporation.

Some Bible towns that the children can learn about include the following:

Jerusalem—where Jesus died
Jericho—where Zacchaeus met Jesus
Nazareth—where Jesus lived with Mary and Joseph
Bethany—where Jesus raised Lazarus from the dead
Emmaus—where two of Jesus' disciples were headed
when He appeared to them
Cana—where Jesus worked His first miracle
Bethlehem—where Jesus was born

The children can locate each of these places on a map of Palestine as it was in the time of Jesus. If the classroom has a wall map, the location of the day's Bible story could be marked with a colorful pushpin. Children need to be reminded that the method of transportation in those days was walking. Even short distances took a long time to cover walking along dusty roads.

It is most helpful to the children if they can draw their own maps that include the towns that Jesus visited. Children remember more when they do something themselves. Many Bibles have a map in the back that can be used as a reference. White paper and colorful marking pens can be used to make attractive maps that will help the children remember Bible places.

Acting Out Bible Stories

Children enjoy acting out Bible stories. Acting is one of the best ways to help children understand the stories. Roleplaying is a good way to act out the stories because the children do not have to memorize lines. The children can portray a story they have heard in class as the teacher rereads it. Shy children should be encouraged, but not forced to participate. They can learn as observers also.

The teacher can assign the roles of various characters in the story. Half the class can roleplay the story while the other half is the audience. Then the groups can switch so that everyone has a chance. The children can roleplay the story several times so that different children can take turns being the various characters. Older children who are able to read can wear character nametags to help the audience keep the characters straight. One class might act out a Bible story for another class.

One of the best Bible stories to roleplay is that of the Good Samaritan (Luke 10:30-37). It has plenty of action that is easily acted out by children. The various actors needed are a traveller, two robbers, a priest, a Levite, a Good Samaritan, and an innkeeper. As the teacher reads the story, the children can portray the traveller being wounded, people passing by him, the Good Samaritan helping him and taking him to the inn. As the children roleplay, they will better understand the story and the actions of those involved. Acting out a Bible story also helps the children remember the story longer.

This and other methods used to guide children in exploring the Bible are good because they involve the students actively in the learning process. These methods help them learn about the good news that Jesus brought to us. The Bible reaffirms God's love for His people.

chapter 8

Reviewing with Games

Games are an excellent way to reinforce what is taught in religious education classes. Games can be used to help children review previously covered material. They also can enhance and enrich a lesson. Games motivate children to want to learn and make learning fun. Games are a good educational tool to use with children because they directly involve the children in the learning process. They provide a much-needed variety of classroom learning experiences.

There are a variety of learning games that can be used by teachers successfully. Some games can be used to promote individual learning. These games are a wonderful, creative means to learning. They allow children to work at their own pace to master the concepts involved. These games allow for concentrated learning in a particular area in which the child needs to improve.

Individual learning games allow the children to take responsibility for their own learning. A great feature of these games is that they have a built-in means of self-checking that allows the children to check their answers immediately and correct mistakes. Thus, the children know right away if they are completing the exercise correctly.

The games can be set up in various learning centers around the room. Rules should be established to facilitate an orderly flow of children and to keep track of who uses each center. Periodically part of the class period could be devoted to the use of these learning centers.

Games that can be used with partners or in small groups help the children encourage each other to learn. They provide opportunities for the children to work together toward the common goal of learning. Often children will feel more at ease with a partner or in a small group than working individually.

Some games involve the whole class. They can provide an excellent review for all the children. These games provide a challenge to the children. They promote a sense of team competition that encourages learning and makes it fun. Games make learning interesting and are a good alternative learning tool.

Following are suggestions for classroom learning games.

Self-Study Flash Cards

This is a good activity for children who need to review terms. Children can work in pairs to help each other learn.

Use index cards for this activity. Each card should have one term on it that the children are to review. The corresponding definition should be on the reverse side of the card.

Two children sit across from each other. The children take turns. One child shows the word to a second child. The second child tells the meaning of the word. The first child states if the answer is correct. If not, the first child tells the correct answer to the other child.

Ideas for types of terms that can be used are the following:

Commandments	God's laws
Apostles	12 friends of Jesus
Bible	Book about God
Prayer	Talking with God
Angels	God's messengers
Christians	People who follow Jesus

New terms can be added to the game as the children study additional concepts. Each game can be stored in a box clearly marked as to the contents. The idea for flash cards is from the book *Lifelines for Religion Teachers* by Sister Anne Cooke, S.S.J.[1]

Match-up Cards

Match-up cards are a great learning tool for children. They are easy to make and very versatile. Match-up cards provide the opportunity for individualized learning that is so important to children.

[1]Sister Anne Cooke, S.S.J., *Lifelines for Religion Teachers* (Mystic, CT.: Twenty-Third Publications, 1977), pp. 14-15. Used by permission of Twenty-Third Publications.

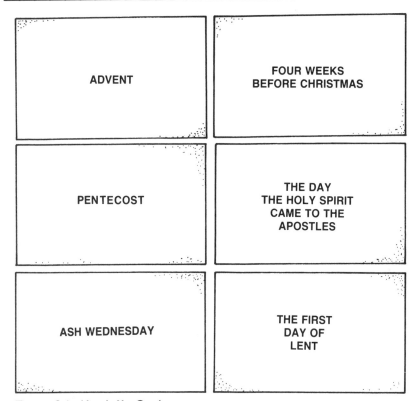

Figure 8-1. Match-Up Cards.

One way to use match-up cards is for reviewing church celebration days. This game helps children remember the names of feasts and seasons and their meanings.

To set up this game use index cards of two colors. On one color cards put the name of a church celebration day that the children should know. On the other color put the corresponding phrase that describes it.

To do this activity, the children place the feast day cards on the left side of a table one underneath the other so that all the cards can be seen. Then the children take the pile of definition cards and place the corresponding meaning to the right of each feast day card (see illustration).

This activity includes a self-checking feature that enables the children to check and correct their work right away for maximum learning. When the cards are made, place a corresponding number on the back of each pair of matching cards. Then when the children have completed the activity, they can turn over the cards and see if the numbers match.

Some celebration days and their definitions that can be used for this game include the following:

Advent	Four weeks before Christmas
Christmas	Jesus' birthday
Ephiphany	The day the Wise Men came to see Jesus
Lent	The 40 days before Easter
Ash Wednesday	The first day of Lent
Holy Thursday	The day of the Last Supper
Good Friday	The day Jesus died on the cross
Easter	The day Jesus rose from the dead
Pentecost	The day the Holy Spirit came to the Apostles

This type of game is an excellent review for children. It can be adapted for many uses. These activities encourage the children to learn. The idea for celebration match-up cards comes from the book *Lifelines for Religion Teachers* by Sister Anne Cooke, S.S.J.[2]

Pantomime

A fun activity for children is pantomime. It involves action, competition, and team spirit. Also it is a good way to review Bible stories. Pantomime involves the entire class in a learning activity.

To play this game divide the class into two teams. Within each team the children should be separated into pairs. The object is for each pair of players to act out a Bible story so that their teammates can guess which story it is. This is accomplished with pantomimed actions. No talking is allowed by those acting out the Bible story.

Have a coffee can filled with slips of paper. On each piece of paper should be the name of a familiar Bible story. Good Bible stories for pantomiming are:

The Cure of the Blind Man	Mark 10:46-52
The Good Shepherd	John 10:11-16
The Good Samaritan	Luke 10:30-37
The Cure of the Lepers	Luke 17:11-19
The Prodigal Son	Luke 15:11-32
The Story of Zacchaeus	Luke 19:1-10
The Cure of the Lame Man	Luke 5:17-26

[2]Cooke, pp. 40-41.

Each team should take turns choosing a slip of paper and pantomiming the story. The pair who will be pantomiming has one minute to discuss privately how they will act out the story.

The two children stand in front of their team and pantomime the story. Their teammates call out guesses until they answer correctly. A time limit should be set. The team getting the most answers in the shortest amount of time wins.

Who Am I?

A game that involves all the children in the class is the "Who Am I?" game. It helps the children review people of God that they have been studying in class. As the children enter the classroom, names of people are taped to the back of their shirts. The children cannot see their names, but they can see those on other children.

The children try to discover their identities by asking questions of the other children that can be answered "yes" or "no." Such questions might be "Was I an Apostle?" or "Did I write the Psalms?" The game continues until all the children have discovered their identities. If some of the children have difficulty, give them hints.

Some people of God that can be used for this game are:

Peter
David
Mary
Moses
Paul
Bartimaeus
Joseph
Matthew

This game helps the children remember facts about biblical people's lives in a way that is fun as well as informative. Children have to review information in their own minds to be able to answer other children's questions as well as ask their own.

Life of Jesus Game

Children can review various events in the life of Jesus through playing a game that involves matching. This game can be played by two or three children.

To make game cards cut eight index cards in half vertically. Print a statement about the life of Jesus on each of eight cards. On the other eight cards print identical statements. Statements that can be used include the following:

> Born in Bethlehem
> Called twelve Apostles
> Cured a lame man
> Told the story of the Prodigal Son
> Taught us the Lord's Prayer
> Said to love one another
> Died on a cross
> Rose on Easter Sunday

The children first mix up the cards. Then they lay out the cards with the statements face down in four rows of four cards. The children take turns turning over any two cards and reading them out loud. If the cards do not match, the player turns them back face down. The children try to remember the cards to make matches.

Each time a match is made, those two cards are removed from the game. The child making the match gets another turn. The game continues until all the cards are matched. This game can be played over and over because each time the cards are in different spaces. The cards can be stored in a small box with directions printed on the top.

Bible People

This activity helps the children to remember which Bible people were in the Old Testament before the coming of Jesus and which were in the New Testament at the time of His coming or after.

To set up this activity use two small boxes. Label one box Old Testament and put a blue dot on it. Label the other box New Testament and put a red dot on it. On index cards print the names of various Bible people that the children have studied. There should be one name on each card. On the backs of the cards with Old Testament names put a blue dot. On the backs of the cards with New Testament names put a red dot.

Some names that can be used for this activity are:

Old Testament	New Testament
Moses	Matthew
Adam	Thomas

Old Testament, cont.

Noah
Isaiah
Abraham
David

New Testament, cont.

Judas
Mary
Peter
Paul

The children classify the Bible names by placing the cards in either the New Testament box or the Old Testament box. When the children have finished, they check the backs of the cards to see if the color dots correspond with the dot on the box. If any cards are in the incorrect category, they should be rearranged.

This activity helps the children to remember to which part of the Bible various biblical figures belong.

Cover-up Game

The cover-up game is designed to help individual children review facts about various people mentioned in the Gospels. The game board is made on an open file folder. Draw lines to divide the board into 12 squares. Each square should contain a fact about one of the Gospel people. Self-adhesive address labels can be used. Type the information

Figure 8-2. Cover-Up Game.

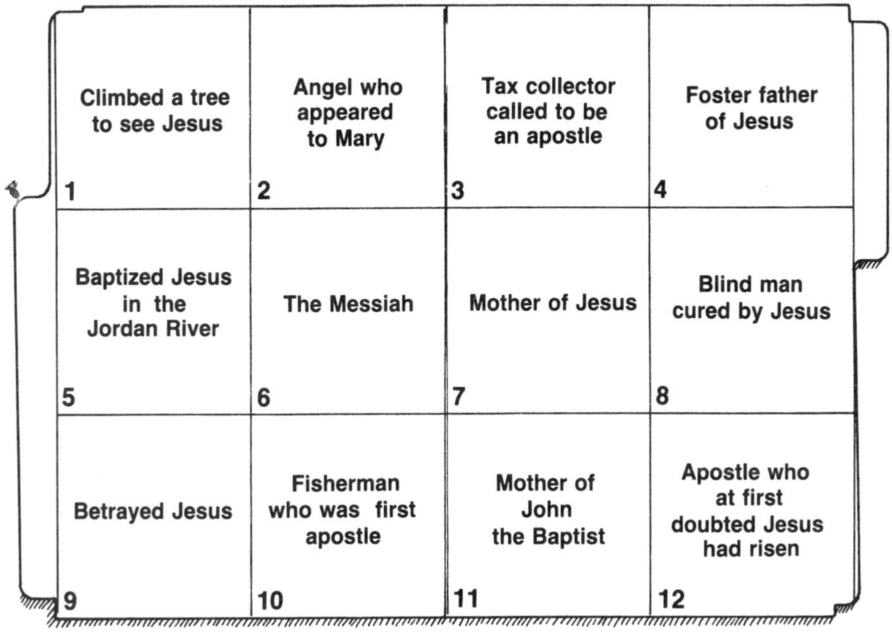

Climbed a tree to see Jesus	Angel who appeared to Mary	Tax collector called to be an apostle	Foster father of Jesus
1	2	3	4
Baptized Jesus in the Jordan River	The Messiah	Mother of Jesus	Blind man cured by Jesus
5	6	7	8
Betrayed Jesus	Fisherman who was first apostle	Mother of John the Baptist	Apostle who at first doubted Jesus had risen
9	10	11	12

onto the labels and place on the board. Put a number in the lower left hand corner of each square to be used for checking purposes (see illustration).

Cut index cards in half to make game cards. Print the name of a Bible person on each card. Self-adhesive labels can also be used for this. On the back of each card put the number used on the square with the corresponding definition.

To play the game, the children place the name cards on top of the corresponding definitions. They can check their answers and rearrange the cards if necessary. Directions for the game should be printed on the outside of the file folder for the children.

The name cards can be placed in an envelope for storage inside the file folder. Mark the envelope with the title of the game in case it becomes separated. Label the game name on the top of the file folder so that it can be easily located in a drawer.

Names and descriptions that can be used are:

Peter	Fisherman who was first Apostle
Zacchaeus	Climbed a tree to see Jesus
John the Baptist	Baptized Jesus in the Jordan River
Mary	Mother of Jesus
Matthew	Tax collector called to be an Apostle
Thomas	Apostle who at first doubted Jesus had risen
Bartimaeus	Blind man cured by Jesus
Gabriel	Angel who appeared to Mary
Elizabeth	Mother of John the Baptist
Joseph	Foster father of Jesus
Judas	Betrayed Jesus
Jesus	The Messiah

This game is an enjoyable challenge for children. They can work alone at their own pace until they feel that they have mastered the information. This game is adapted from the book *File Folder Learning Centers for Bible Study Fun* by Donna Skinner.[3]

Bible Quotes

Learning to look up references in the Bible is a skill that must be practiced to be learned. Mastery of the skill comes only after practice.

---

[3]From *File Folder Learning Centers for Bible Study Fun* © 1982. The Standard Publishing Company, Cincinnati, Ohio, pp. 63-71. Division of Standex International Corporation. Used by permission.

Matching Bible quotes provides the opportunity for children to work at their own individual pace. In this activity the children match Bible references to quotes. The teachers are available to work with the children on a one-to-one basis.

To prepare the game, print a Bible quote on each of five index cards. Cut off the flaps from five small letter envelopes. On the envelopes print the matching Bible references. Pin the envelopes to a bulletin board. To complete the activity the children must look up the reference in the Bible. Then they place the index card bearing the quoted words in the envelope.

Some quotations that can be used are:

This is my commandment: love one another as I have loved you.	John 15:12
I am the Good Shepherd, I know my own and my own know me.	John 10:14
In the beginning God created the heavens and the earth.	Genesis 1:1
And know that I am with you always, yes, to the end of time.	Matthew 28:20
Clap your hands, all you peoples, acclaim God with shouts of joy.	Psalm 47:1

It is very important to be sure that the quotes used are from the Bible translation that the children use to look for them. Otherwise it can be very confusing and frustrating.

Bulletin boards for this and other activities can be made inexpensively in a few minutes from dressmaker cutting boards available at fabric stores. Cover one side with a large piece of burlap and tape or staple the edges to the back.

Sorting Game

This is a game that the children can play individually to help them remember facts about people they should know. The sorting game is a challenge because there is more than one right answer. Matching phrases describing people to the correct person is the object of the game. This game can be used with Bible people as the subject.

To set up the game cut off the flaps from four stationery envelopes. Glue the envelopes to the inside of an open file folder turned sideways. On each envelope print the name of one Bible figure about whom the children have studied. On each envelope also write a number in the bottom left-hand corner.

Prepare the game cards using index cards. Each card should have one statement about one of the Bible figures. The cards need to be numbered on the reverse side. Corresponding numbers enable the children to check if they have matched the correct description to the right person.

To play the game the children place the cards in the correct envelopes. There should be several statements about each Bible person. Directions for this game should be put on the outside of the file folder. This allows the children to work independently and to know what is expected of them.

Suggestions for Bible people that can be used with this game and matching phrases follow:

Peter   First Apostle called
Also called Simon
Denied Jesus three times
Mother-in-law cured by Jesus
Fisherman

Mary   Mother of Jesus
With Jesus at Cana
Saw the angel Gabriel
Cousin to Elizabeth

Jesus   Cured lame men and lepers
Told us to love God and our neighbor
The Savior who died on the cross
Told parables
Said that He was the Good Shepherd

Paul   Also called Saul
At first persecuted Christians
Blinded on the road to Damascus
Wrote part of the New Testament

When the children are finished, they should check the numbers to see if their answers are correct. If not, they should move the cards until all the descriptions match the correct person. Games such as this enhance learning. They provide an interesting method of review and make learning enjoyable.

Board Games

Board games are a fun way for children to review previously covered material. They can be played by several children at one time.

The pattern for the game board is made by sticking colored self-adhesive circles onto an open file folder. The pattern forms the path

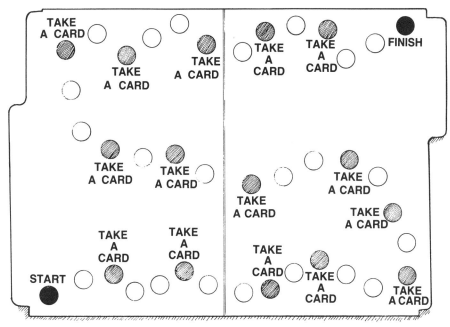

Figure 8-3. Board Game.

for the children's markers to follow from Start to Finish (see illustration). The players throw a die to tell how many spaces to move.

Some of the circles should be a second color. When the players land on one of these circles, they pick a card from the question pile. If they answer the question correctly, they move forward one space. If their answer is incorrect, they move backward one space. More than one player can occupy the same space at the same time. The first player to finish wins the game.

To prepare question cards use index cards. The questions should cover the material that the children have been studying. The easiest way is to type the questions on self-adhesive address labels. Then peel off the backing and place each question on an index card. Answers should be placed in the same manner on the back of each card. Place the question cards in a pile with the question side up.

Some questions that could be used in a review game of this type are:

Who was the mother of Jesus?	(Mary)
In what town was Jesus born?	(Bethlehem)
Who wrote the Psalms?	(David)

What job did Peter have before he became an Apostle?	(fisherman)
On what day does Lent begin?	(Ash Wednesday)
What are God's laws called?	(Ten Commandments)

Directions for playing the game should be put on the front of the file folder. The title of each game should be put on the tab of the folder. These games can be easily folded up to store in a drawer. The question cards, markers, and die can be placed in small plastic bags attached to the file folders.

Many different games can be made using this method. The pattern and color of the circles can be varied with each game. A separate group of questions should be used for each game. A game could be made for each unit of study or for each Bible story the children learn.

The game boards and question cards can be covered with clear adhesive paper for durability. There should be one game for about every four to six children. These games are a good way for children to review information. They are fun to play and can be used successfully to reinforce learning. The idea for board games made from file folders comes from the article "Board Games for Review Can Be Made Easily From Everyday File Folders" by Donn P. McGuirk in *Church Teachers Magazine*.[4]

Clue Game

A good method of review for the entire class is the clue game. It can be used to review a particular unit of study or as a general review. This game is similar to a spelling bee. It provides a more interesting means of review than writing answers to questions.

Prepare a list of questions dealing with what the children have been studying in class. Divide the children into two teams—Team A and Team B. Have each team stand along the walls on either side of the classroom.

Ask the first question of the first person on Team A. In order to remain standing, that person must answer the question correctly. If the answer is incorrect, that person sits down. Then it is the turn of the first person on Team B. That person is asked a question. It is a different question unless Team A missed. Then Team B must correctly answer

[4]Donn P. McGuirk, "Board Games For Review Can Be Made Easily From Everyday File Folders," *Church Teachers Magazine*, 10, No. 4 (January/February 1983), pp. 143-44. Used by permission.

the original question. The winning team is the one with the most people left standing.

Some questions that could be asked in the clue game are:

What prayer did Jesus give us?	(Lord's Prayer)
To whom did God give the Ten Commandments?	(Moses)
What man climbed a tree to see Jesus?	(Zacchaeus)
What is the four weeks before Christmas called?	(Advent)
What town did Jesus enter on Palm Sunday?	(Jerusalem)
What are the twelve followers of Jesus called?	(Apostles)

Games are an important tool in religious education because they reinforce learning and make it fun. They can be easily adapted to a particular unit of study where needed and help children remember what they have learned.

chapter 9

Giving Thanks
at Thanksgiving

Thanksgiving offers us a wonderful opportunity to thank God for all He has given us. It is a time when we pause to remember our many blessings and from Whom they came. We must be sure that Thanksgiving means giving thanks to our Creator who gave us our world and all the people in it who love and care for us.

Thanksgiving is a time when families and friends gather together and share a meal as members of God's family. It is a time to listen to one another and to share a sense of belonging. It is also a time to share ourselves with others and to remember that we are God's gift to one another.

Many of the children in our classes will have seen preparations going on at home and in stores for Thanksgiving. We can help them see the tradition of Thanksgiving as a celebration of God's presence in their lives. Also we can encourage their interest in and enthusiasm for holidays to help them learn about their relationship with God. The children should come to see celebration as a natural part of God's gift of life.

Hopefully, the holiday lessons and activities will be long remembered by the children. Every year when they see Thanksgiving preparations being made, they will think of giving thanks to God who made it all possible. Thus, the lesson will live on and on.

Following are some ways to help the children learn about the meaning of Thanksgiving as a time of thanking God.

The First Thanksgiving

We can begin by explaining to the children the origin of the Thanksgiving holiday. Children like to hear how customs began. It helps them to understand holidays and their meaning.

Explain to them that the first Thanksgiving was held in 1621 by people called the Pilgrims. They were early settlers of the eastern United States who had come from Europe, far across the Atlantic Ocean, to live in a new land. The Pilgrims settled in Plymouth, Massachusetts.

The Pilgrims decided to have a celebration that year because they wanted to thank God for the first year's successful harvest. They invited the local Indians to join them for a Thanksgiving feast that lasted three days. Now each year we continue the custom of celebrating Thanksgiving as a time of giving thanks to God for all His gifts.

Allow the opportunity for the children to ask questions about the story and the times. It is difficult for them to imagine life more than 300 years ago.

Traditions

Encourage the children to tell the class about their Thanksgiving traditions at home. Sometimes they need to be asked questions to guide the class discussion such as these:

> Are you having company for Thanksgiving dinner?
> Will you be going to your grandparents' house?
> Will you see many of your relatives?
> Do you go to church on Thanksgiving morning?
> Do you do something special every Thanksgiving?
> Who will say grace?
> What will you eat for Thanksgiving dinner?
> Will you have turkey and pumpkin pie?
> What will everyone do after dinner?

Children learn from one another as well as the teachers. The children can find out a great deal about Thanksgiving traditions by listening to their classmates. The variety of customs that they hear about helps them to realize that different people do things in different ways. This awareness helps the children learn to respect other people's ideas and ways of doing things.

It is important for the children to have the chance to contribute to the class discussion. Contributing builds self-esteem and a sense of purpose. Children feel like worthwhile human beings when they have something to say and others listen to them. It makes them feel important and they are.

Thank You Collage

The children can make a thank you collage to help them think of things for which they can be thankful at Thanksgiving time. All of us tend to take things for granted unless we do stop to count our many blessings.

On a large piece of posterboard print the words "Thank You God." Have an assortment of pictures cut from magazines on a table. Pictures can include people, families, foods, sunsets, trees, flowers, and animals.

Each child should be encouraged to choose a picture for the collage of something that God gave us. Have more pictures available than the number of children so that the child who chooses last really does have a choice.

Then the children can glue their pictures onto the poster to make a collage. This class activity helps the children realize that God has given us many gifts. The bright, colorful collage can then be displayed in the classroom as a reminder of God's gifts.

Prayer Turkeys

This activity puts giving thanks to God on a personal level for the children. It helps them become aware of the good things in their lives for which they can be truly thankful.

The children cut turkey shapes out of brown construction paper. Then they cut four feathers for each turkey out of different colors of construction paper such as blue, yellow, green, and orange. The feathers are glued onto the turkeys. Both the turkeys and feathers should be precut for younger children to assemble.

On the body of the turkey the words "Thank You God for . . ." can be printed by the children. Then on each feather they print something for which they are thankful. Younger children can dictate to the teachers (see illustration).

This activity has meaning for the children only if the ideas printed on the feathers are the children's own. If all the turkeys say the same things, it has become the teacher's project and not the children's. We have to provide the opportunity for children to learn by doing themselves.

The prayers on the turkeys can be used for a Thanksgiving grace or a bedtime prayer. Prayer turkeys can be displayed at home on the refrigerator or bulletin board as a reminder to all to give thanks to God at Thanksgiving.

Figure 9-1. Prayer Turkey.

Hand Turkeys

The turkey has become the symbol of Thanksgiving. The Pilgrims probably had wild turkeys for dinner on the first Thanksgiving. Children enjoy making colorful turkeys out of their own hand shapes.

This project can be accomplished by most children all by themselves, which makes them feel special. They like to use their hands for the pattern because their hands are part of themselves.

Direct the children to draw the outline of one of their hands on a piece of white paper. The outline can be drawn with a crayon of any color that the children choose. The teachers may want to illustrate this procedure on the blackboard.

The children's thumbs become the turkeys' heads. An eye can be added to each turkey. The children's palms are the turkeys' bodies. Legs and feet should be drawn underneath the turkeys' bodies. The children's fingers are the turkeys' feathers and can be brightly colored.

Hand turkeys can be hung around the room to give it a festive look to help celebrate the holiday.

Thank You Notes

This idea helps the children learn to say thank you to those people in their lives who love, care for, and help them. Thank you notes are a good Thanksgiving tradition that can be done year after year.

Explain to the children that it is not enough to know that they are thankful, they must also express that thanks to the important people in their lives. Discuss with the children to whom they might send thank you notes. Encourage them to think especially of people who might not receive any other Thanksgiving greeting. Each child needs to make an individual decision.

A variety of art supplies should be available to the children for this project. A half sheet of paper can be folded in half to make a thank you note. Children can draw around a turkey-shaped cookie cutter on the front of the card. Then they can use crayons or markers to add details if they wish.

Inside each card should be a short note of thanks to the person for whom the note is intended and the child's signature. Older children can write their own messages. Younger children can tell the teacher what to write for them.

Instead of individual cards, the children can all work together on one large thank you note for the pastor or someone special. To do this use a large piece of posterboard folded in half. Divide the front of the card into as many squares as there are children in the class. Each child can draw something for which to be thankful inside one of the squares.

Inside the card should be the words "Happy Thanksgiving." Let the children sign their names under this greeting. Each child can choose one color crayon or marker for the picture and signature. This makes a wonderful card of which the children can be proud. As a class they can go together to present their card to the pastor or someone special.

Food Collection

Thanksgiving is a good time to take up a canned goods collection for those in need. We need to remember those who have not been as fortunate as we have been.

We should explain to the children that not everyone will be having a big Thanksgiving dinner. Some people who are out of work do not have enough money to buy everything that they need. Tell the children that because we are all members of God's family, we are to help others.

Ask the children to each bring a can, jar, or package of food to class the following week. Send home a list of appropriate foods that are nonperishable and nutritious. Such foods include:

Peanut butter
Macaroni and cheese
Tuna
Canned vegetables
Pork and beans
Applesauce
Canned chili
Rice
Dry milk
Baby food

Many churches have a food pantry where food is given out to those in need. Find out which food items are needed most at the current time. Many local charities also distribute food to people who do not have enough to eat. Call them to be sure and to find out if the food needs to be delivered or if they will pick it up.

Have cardboard cartons ready for the children in the classrooms. The children can put their food items in the boxes and the food will be ready for delivery or pick up. Have extra cans of food for the children who did not bring theirs so they will have something to contribute.

These collections usually net a great deal of food if all the classes participate. It is amazing what people can do together.

Blackboard Prayer

To show appreciation for God's gifts, the children can compose and say a prayer of thanks. On the blackboard print the words "Thanksgiving Prayer." If a blackboard is not available, a piece of posterboard can be used. Explain to the children that they are going to write a prayer.

As the children name things for which they are thankful, draw a simple picture on the blackboard and put the word underneath. When all the children who want to participate have done so, the pictures or words can be read as a prayer.

Together the children should say the name of each gift and add the refrain "Thank You God." The prayer can be like this one:

For sunshine,
Thank You God.
For flowers,
Thank You God.
For squirrels,
Thank You God.
For pets,
Thank You God.
For families,
Thank You God.
For Your love,
Thank You God.

Thanksgiving Feast

The children can celebrate Thanksgiving in the classroom as a community of His people. Each child should bring something for this celebration. Suitable items could be raisins, popcorn, cookies, apples, juice, cups, plates, and napkins. Notes should go home the week before so that the parents will be aware of what the children should bring.

It makes children feel proud to contribute to a class project such as this. The children should pass out the items that they brought to their classmates. Be sure to have extra supplies on hand for the child who forgets. This way the party can go on and the child's feelings will be spared. The children can say a short prayer before they begin eating. Celebrations make learning fun for all the children.

Pilgrim Hats

The children will enjoy making Pilgrim hats to wear either to their Thanksgiving feast or at home. Since the Pilgrims celebrated the first Thanksgiving, Pilgrim hats are an appropriate symbol.

Black construction paper is used to make the hats. Cut out the shape of a tall hat with a brim from the paper. Also cut out a strip of black paper to use as the back brim of the hat. Staple the two pieces together. Each hat should have a white hatband and an orange paper buckle glued on the front for a finished look. Young children can assemble hats from precut pieces (see illustration).

The children look great in these hats. Provide mirrors so that they can see how they look as Pilgrims.

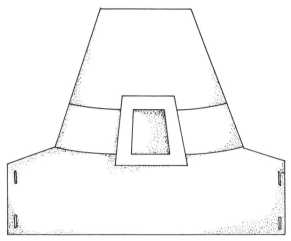

Figure 9-2. Pilgrim Hat.

Party Placemats

The children can make placemats to use at their class party or at home. Each child should pick out a piece of any color construction paper. The placemats can be decorated with crayons or markers. The children can draw things for which they are thankful. This is a means of expressing gratitude for God's gifts without words.

Then show the children how to fringe the edges of their placemats with scissors. Half-inch cuts can be made all around the edges. The placemats can be covered with clear, self-adhesive plastic.

These placemats can be used under the children's plates and cups to give the table a festive look. They are thus practical as well as decorative.

Thanksgiving Prayer Service

A Thanksgiving prayer service offers the children the opportunity to thank God for His many gifts. All the classes can come together in praise and thanksgiving. A prayer service helps the children to express their feelings to God who made everything possible.

A ceremony such as the following can be used. It comes from *Liturgies for Little Ones* by Carol Rezy[1] A beginning and ending song could be added to allow the children to thank God in this way also. Children can be chosen to act as readers of assigned parts.

[1]Carol Rezy, *Liturgies for Little Ones* (Notre Dame, Indiana: Ave Maria Press, 1978), pp. 53-54. Used by permission.

THEME:

Thursday is a special day! It is Thanksgiving! It's the day we thank God for all the things He has given us. Think of all the things we can be thankful for: our families and friends, our food and clothes, our school and teachers, and all the love in the world. Let's celebrate our thanks to God today . . .

RESPONSORIAL PSALM: Ps 136:1,4-6,7-9,25-26 (paraphrased)

Refrain: GIVE THANKS TO THE LORD FOR HE IS GOOD!

Give thanks to the Lord for He is good. He made the heavens, the earth, and the waters.
He performs great things. He made the great lights—the sun, the moon and the stars.
He gives us all we need. He loves us forever! Give thanks to our God! He loves us forever.

GOSPEL: Lk 17:11-17 (paraphrased)

On His way to Jerusalem, Jesus entered one of the villages. He met 10 lepers. They called to him, "Jesus! Master! Have pity on us!" As they went away, they were cured. One of them came back and praised God at the top of his voice. He knelt in front of Jesus and thanked him. This made Jesus say, "Were not all ten made clean? Where are the other nine? It seems that no one has come back to give praise to God, except this one."

PETITIONS:

Response: LORD, HEAR OUR PRAYER!

That we always remember to thank God for all the things he has given us, we pray to the Lord.
For all the people in the world who do not have the gifts that we share here today, we pray to the Lord.
For all the sick, poor, and lonely people. Fill them with your love and happiness on this Thanksgiving Day, we pray to the Lord.

PREPARATION OF GIFTS:

We take up a picture of a family. God gives us our family and friends to love.

We also take up a basket of food. God always takes care of us. He gives us the things we need.

To show that we are thankful for all God's gifts, we take up a big "THANK YOU" sign to put on the altar.

This type of ceremony helps the children to give thanks at Thanksgiving.

chapter 10

Celebrating the Christmas Season

The season of Advent allows us time to prepare ourselves for the coming of Jesus at Christmas. These four weeks are a time of anticipation and of waiting. They are a time of joy and a time of hope.

After thousands of years God was fulfilling His promise to send a Savior to His people. "Yes, God loved the world so much that he gave his only Son" (John 3:16). Christmas is a celebration of love—the love of God for us and the love we should have for other people. Advent should be a time when we grow in love.

Advent is a time to reach out to others. It is a beginning. We must learn to live the spirit of love and hope of the Advent season throughout the year. The love that came into the world on the first Christmas should be a light to guide all people to Jesus.

Christmas is a time of rejoicing. We should celebrate the great feast with hearts filled with gladness. The Messiah has come. The angels proclaimed the good news to the shepherds on that first Christmas. So in our own lives we should share the joyous tidings with others.

We can help the children to experience the great joy that this season brings by enriching their lives with the good news of God's love. Activities that can be used to help children discover the message of hope of the Christmas season follow.

Waiting

The time of Advent can be explained to the children as a time of waiting. Let them name things that they wait for in their lives such as grandparents coming to visit, dinner to be ready, and the coming of their birthdays.

113

Explain to the children that Advent is the four weeks before Christmas. We are to use this time to get ready for Jesus. Have the children name some of the ways that they and their families get ready for Christmas. Some of the ways that they might name include the following:

Trimming the tree
Hanging up stockings
Wrapping gifts
Sending cards
Putting up outdoor lights
Singing carols
Decorating the house
Baking cookies

Let the children know that Advent is also a time to get ready on the inside for the coming of Jesus. It is a time to grow in the love of God. We must prepare our hearts for Jesus' coming at Christmas.

The season of Advent is very long for children because it is filled with anticipation. Learning about the reason that we make all the preparations helps them to use it as a time to learn about God.

Advent Wreath

One of the most popular and meaningful Advent customs is the lighting of the Advent wreath. This is a circle of green holding four candles. The circular form represents God's unending love for His people. The green is a symbol of hope. The four candles represent the four weeks of Christmas. They also symbolize the thousands of years that people waited for the Messiah to come.

The first week of Advent one candle is lit. The second week two candles are lit. The third week three candles are lit. The fourth week all the candles are lit. Following the lighting of the candles, a prayer is said. The children can hold hands and form a circle around the Advent wreath for the lighting of the candles.

A different prayer can be said each week around the Advent wreath. The prayers should reflect the spirit of love and hope that is the Advent season. They should express to God our longing for His Son. Prayers such as the following can be said:

First Week. Dear God, as we begin this Advent season help us to prepare to welcome Jesus with love. Amen.

Second week. Dear God, You created each of us and gave us this world full of beauty and wonder. Then you sent Jesus to help us. May we show our love for You every day of our lives. Amen.

Third week. Dear God, our hearts are filled with joy at the coming of Jesus. May we share our joy with others this Christmas season. Amen.

Fourth week. Dear God, thank you for sending Jesus to us. May we always follow Him in everything we do. Bless us and our families and friends this Christmas season. Amen.

Advent Chain

The children can make Advent chains to help them count the days until Christmas. This makes the waiting easier. It is also a good way to see how long it is until Christmas comes.

Strips of paper can be taped together to form a chain with interlocking links. There should be one link for each day remaining until Christmas. Each day at home the children can take a link off of the chain. When the last link is removed, it is Christmas.

Part of the Christmas story can be written on each link to tell the story. These can be duplicated ahead of time with one set for each child to assemble. The Christmas story can be told the following way. Each sentence is for one link. They are based on the Gospel accounts of the birth of Jesus:

God sent the angel Gabriel to a young woman named Mary in the town of Nazareth.
The angel told Mary that she was to be the mother of Jesus.
Gabriel also told Mary that her cousin, Elizabeth, would have a child.
Mary said yes to God.
Mary went to visit her cousin, Elizabeth.
Mary stayed with Elizabeth for three months and then went home.
Elizabeth had a son named John.
Caesar Augustus ordered a census of the whole world.
Mary and Joseph travelled to Bethlehem for the census.
In Bethlehem there was no room for them at the inn.
Mary and Joseph stayed in a stable.
In the stable in Bethlehem Jesus was born on the first Christmas.
In the countryside there were shepherds watching their sheep.
An angel came to tell the shepherds that Jesus was born.
The shepherds went to see Jesus in the stable at Bethlehem.
The shepherds went back to their flocks praising God.

Saint Nicholas

The story of Saint Nicholas, the first Santa Claus, is a good one to tell the children at Christmas time. His story captures the spirit of giving. His feast day is celebrated on December 6.

Saint Nicholas was a bishop in the country of Lycia in the fourth century. Stories about him have been told throughout the centuries. Many of them concern his generosity to the poor.

The best known legend is that he provided the dowries for the three daughters of a poor man. He tossed a bag of gold coins through the window of the man's house three times so that his daughters could be married. St. Nicholas did this at night in secret. Thus, the custom of giving gifts on his feast day evolved.

Secret Friend

A fun activity during Advent is having a secret friend. Put all of the children's names on slips of paper in a jar. Have each child pick the name of a secret friend. If some of the children draw their own names, they should put their names back in the jar and draw again.

The idea is that the children do good deeds for their secret friends during Advent. Before the drawing let the children discuss the type of things that they might do for their secret friends. This will give the children ideas. One child could write a note to another and sign it "your secret friend." The note could tell something nice about the person and could be on that child's desk before class. Another idea is to give a secret friend an unusual rock for a collection. One secret friend could bring another an apple.

The identity of the secret friends should not be revealed until the last class before Christmas. The secrecy is part of what makes this project fun. If the children are having a gift exchange in class, they should bring a gift for the person whose name they drew.

Jesse Tree

The Jesse tree is a learning activity that helps the children learn about Jesus' family tree. His heritage is represented by symbols of His ancestors. The idea for the Jesse tree comes from the prophecy of Isaiah (11:1): "A shoot springs from the stock of Jesse . . ." A thousand years later Jesus was born into this family.

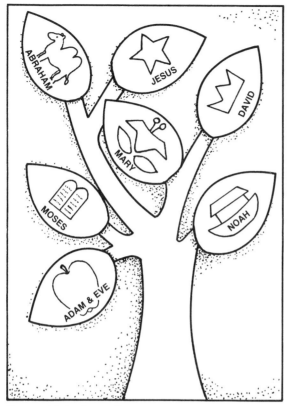

Figure 10-1. Jesse Tree.

The Jesse tree can be done as either a class project or an individual one. A large tree trunk and branches cut from posterboard can be pinned to the bulletin board. Each child can be assigned an ancestor for which to make a symbol. The children can place their symbols on the tree one by one and tell what they represent. For a class that meets daily, one child can be assigned each day during Advent to place a symbol on the tree.

The children can make individual paper Jesse trees. A brown trunk and branches can be cut from construction paper and glued to a sheet of white construction paper. Symbols can be drawn on green leaf shapes cut from paper. Then the leaves can be glued to the tree branches (see illustration).

Some of Jesus' ancestors and appropriate symbols are:

Adam and Eve (apple): Adam and Eve were the first people of God's creation.
Noah (ark): Noah was a person of great faith. He followed God's will in all things.
Abraham (camel): Abraham was told to leave his country and set out for a new land. He did as God asked.
Moses (ten commandments): At Mount Sinai Moses received the laws of God. He told the people to obey God.
David (crown): David was annointed King of Israel. His father was Jesse.
Mary (lily): Mary said yes to God. She became the mother of Jesus. She lived a life of love.
Jesus (star): Jesus is the long-awaited Messiah. He is the Son of God. A star shone over the stable on the first Christmas.

Bread Dough Ornaments

Bread dough ornaments are easy and inexpensive to make. The children can make them for Christmas gifts for family members or friends.

The dough is made from 2 cups of flour, ½ cup of salt, and ¾ cup of water mixed together in a bowl. This can be done ahead of time.

The children can roll out the dough with a rolling pin on a floured table. They can make wreaths, bells, and other holiday ornaments. Use plastic cookie cutters that leave impressions in the dough. Older children may want to mold their ornaments rather than roll them.

Each ornament should have a hairpin pushed in the top to form a hangar. Bake the ornaments in a 250 degree oven for about two hours or until a pin cannot be pushed through the ornament. Molded ornaments are usually thicker and take more baking time.

At the next class period the children can paint their ornaments in holiday colors. When the paint is dry, a coat of clear polyurethane will give the ornaments a finished look.

Wrapping Paper

Children will enjoy making their own Christmas wrapping paper. Large sheets of white newsprint are excellent for this project. Potato prints in bright Christmas colors can be stamped on the paper in a random design by the children.

A large potato can be used for two shapes if cut in half. Make a raised symbol on the cut edge of the potato by cutting away the excess around the edges. Shapes such as stars, trees, and bells are good Christmas designs.

The children should wear paint shirts for this project. To make the wrapping paper, they dip the potato into tempra paint and stamp the design on the paper. Red and green are good Christmas paint colors. The children might stamp a red bell several times and then a green tree shape on their wrapping paper. Allow a few minutes for the wrapping paper to dry.

Potato prints make lovely, personal gift wrap. The children feel proud of their ability and a part of Christmas preparations when they make their own wrapping paper.

Paper Wreaths

Encourage the children to look beyond their immediate family and friends at Christmas time. Remind them that Jesus brought a message of love and caring.

A lovely service project is making paper wreaths for every person's door at the local nursing home. Check with the activity director at the nursing home to secure permission for this project before beginning.

Lovely wreaths can be made from red and green construction paper. Cut out a wreath shape from green construction paper. A red paper bow can be cut out for each wreath from red construction paper.

Figure 10-2. Paper Wreath.

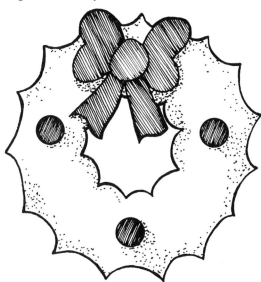

Glue the bow to the top of the wreath. Small red paper circles can be glued to the wreath to look like holly berries (see illustration).

The wreaths can be secured to each resident's door with masking tape. This also makes them easy to remove after Christmas. If possible, take the children when the wreaths are put up on the doors.

The nursing home halls look so cheery when each resident's door is decorated with its own Christmas wreath. This type of project gives the children a way to reach out and help others in the Christmas season. This idea was previously published in my article "Advent Family Day" in *Today's Parish* magazine.[1]

Snowflakes

The children can decorate their own classrooms with paper snowflakes hung from the ceiling. Explain to the children that God made each individual snowflake unique and different just like them. Encourage them to use their creativity so each child's creation will turn out a little different from anyone else's.

White typing or duplicating paper can be used to make snow-flakes. Cut the paper to form a square. Then each paper is folded in half and then in half again. Use the scissors to round off one point into a wide curve. Then fold in half again to make a triangle.

The children use their scissors to cut triangular-shaped pieces from the three sides. When the paper is unfolded, a snowflake has been formed. The children will be very pleased and surprised to see what they made.

The snowflakes should be hung from the ceiling with string to decorate the classroom. Be sure each snowflake has the creator's name on it so that the children can take them home at a later class time.

Trimming a Tree

A wonderful idea for celebrating the joy of the Christmas season is to trim a Christmas tree for the hallway. This adds a festive touch to the classroom area. An artificial tree can be used year after year and does not present a fire hazard.

The tree can be a joint project of all the classes. Each group can add ornaments during their classtime. Start early enough in the season

[1]Previously published in the October 1983 issue of *Today's Parish*, p. 20, a magazine of ministry and management for parish leaders, published by Twenty-Third Publications, P.O. Box 180, Mystic, CT 06355.

so that the children will have the opportunity to see the fully decorated tree. Ornaments made by the children themselves make this project more meaningful. Inexpensive ornaments can be made with felt, sequins, and glue.

Wreaths can be cut from green felt and decorated with a red felt bow. Red sequins add a sparkle to these ornaments. Stockings can be cut from red felt and decorated with a strip of white felt on the top, heel, and toe of each ornament. Gold sequins make these ornaments special. Green felt bells can ring out the glad tidings. These can be decorated with a strip of red felt across the middle and gold sequins.

The ornaments can be hung from the tree by the children with ornament hangars. Allow the glue to dry for a few minutes first. Each of the children's names should be on the back of the ornaments. Use a strip of masking tape for a name label. The children can take their ornaments home just before Christmas to decorate their families' trees.

The decorated tree is a joyful reminder of the Christmas season and also helps the children to feel a part of the preparations.

Gift Certificates

We need to emphasize to the children that gift-giving at Christmas does not have to mean store-bought gifts. The best gift is always the gift of oneself. Encourage the children to give gift certificates to their family members for Christmas.

Gift certificate forms can be handmade by the individual children or they can be duplicated on bright green paper. There should be blanks for the children to fill in the name of the person for whom the certificate is intended, a place for the children to sign their names, and a space for the favor offered (see illustration).

The favor must be one the child is willing to perform and one suitable to the person who is receiving it. Some of the types of favors that can be offered are:

I will make your bed on the morning of your choice.
I will shine your shoes for church.
I will play your favorite game one time with you.
I will let you borrow anything of mine for one day.
I will set the table for dinner on the night of your choice.

Provide envelopes for the gift certificates so that the favor will remain a secret until Christmas. The envelopes can be placed on the Christmas tree at home to be opened on Christmas morning.

TO _____

FROM _____

THIS CERTIFICATE ENTITLES YOU TO _____

_____

MERRY CHRISTMAS

Figure 10-3. Gift Certificate.

Talk to the children about the custom of giving gifts. Explain that we give gifts at Christmas because we are full of joy because Jesus came and we want to share that joy with others.

Toy Collection

To encourage the children to give at Christmas time and not just receive, initiate a toy collection. Many charities and organizations collect toys for those in need at Christmas. Check with one of them for the type of gifts needed and whether or not they should be wrapped. Also make arrangements for delivering the gifts to the organization responsible.

Explain the project to the children and send home a note with a reminder of the details. Encourage the children to help to select the gift and to help pay for it. Make them aware of the need. Explain that we are giving these gifts in remembrance of Jesus' birthday.

On the day of the toy collection the children can place their gifts in an assigned spot such as under the Christmas tree. Thank them for helping to make someone else's Christmas brighter.

Christmas Cards

The custom of sending cards to others at Christmas evolved as one way to share the joy and hope of the Christmas season with others. Children can make Christmas cards for their families, for each other, or as a service project.

Lovely cards can be made with construction paper. Cut pieces of construction paper in half and then fold in half. The front of the cards can be decorated with symbols cut from other pieces of construction paper. Stencil books can be a terrific help in making symbols or provide cardboard patterns to draw around and cut out for the cards. Each child should be free to choose a symbol.

Appropriate Christmas symbols for cards include the following:

Star
Wreath
Holly
Candle
Ornament
Gift box
Angel
Snowflake
Tree
Bell

On the inside of the card a Christmas message can be written and then the children can sign their names. These cards stand up and can be displayed anywhere as a sign of the Christmas season and the joy it brings.

Loving Hands Wreath

An appropriate classroom door decoration that carries out the theme of helping others is the loving hands wreath. This wreath uses handshapes from all the children in the class.

Draw around each child's hand on green construction paper. The children should print their names on their handshapes and then cut them out of the paper. The teacher should help the children arrange the handshapes in an overlapping manner to form a wreath. The fingers should point outwards.

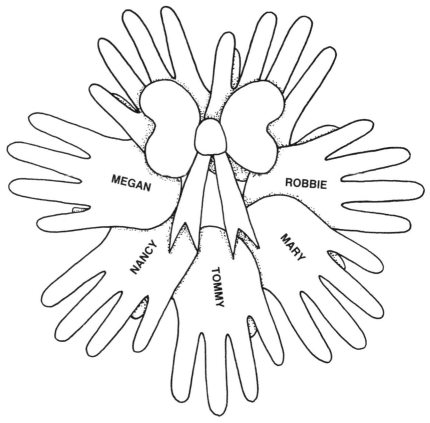

Figure 10-4. Loving Hands Wreath.

Glue each hand to the next one on the wreath. Then cut out a big red paper bow and glue on the top of the wreath for a decorative touch (see illustration).

This wreath helps the children remember to use their hands to help others and shows them what they can accomplish if they all work together. This idea is from *The Big Book of Bible Crafts and Projects* by Joy Mackenzie.[2]

Arrangement of the Creche

A creche scene with the figures of Jesus, Mary, Joseph, angels, shepherds, and animals in a stable can help the children understand the story of the first Christmas.

[2]Joy Mackenzie, *The Big Book of Bible Crafts and Projects* (Nashville, TN: Impact Books, 1981, reassigned to The Zondervan Corporation, Grand Rapids, MI, 1982), p. 144. Used by permission of The Zondervan Corporation.

The children will learn from arranging the creche scene themselves. Each child can be given one of the figures to put in place. The children should come forward one by one. The children should tell the significance of their individual figures. The teacher can read a narration for younger children. Cardboard figures are available in card shops that are inexpensive and will not break if young children drop them.

The following narration can be read:

The Stable. I was hidden away in darkness far from the noise and lights of Bethlehem. But Mary and Joseph noticed me . . . They brought Jesus to me. On that first Christmas night this lonely stable became the most important place on the earth.

The Donkey. I carried Mary to Bethlehem . . . When we came to the stable, this tired, hungry donkey enjoyed his rest. My passengers were safe. My job was done.

The Animals. We are the animals who made our home in the stable. How glad we were to share our roof with God's own Son . . .

Joseph. I am Joseph. God chose me to care for Jesus and Mary. I tried hard to find a safe, warm place for Mary, my wife, to stay . . . The birth of Jesus filled that poor stable with happiness and peace.

Mary. I am Mary. God chose me to be the mother of Jesus, His Son . . . I knew the whole world was waiting for Jesus. I longed to share my Son with everyone.

The Star. I am the star whose light filled the sky on the night that Jesus was born. My great brightness announced: The Light of the World has come.

The Angel. I am the angel who sang to the shepherds: 'I bring you good news of great joy. Today your Savior is born.'

The Shepherds. We were Jesus' first visitors . . . But holding Him brought us such hope and happiness, we knew the angels had spoken the truth: The world would never look the same to us again.

The Infant in the Manger. I am Jesus. Just as I came to Bethlehem on that first Christmas night, I long to come to your house today . . . Share your Christmas love and joy together, and you will know that I am here.

This ceremony may be appropriately concluded by singing Christmas carols such as "Away in a Manger" and "Silent Night." Doing the creche arrangement in this way involves the children in the learning process. They will be more likely to comprehend the significance of the creche scene and the whole Christmas message. This ceremony is condensed from "Arrangement of the Creche" by Carol Clark in *Religion Teacher's Journal.*[3]

[3]Carol Clark, "Arrangement of the Creche," *Religion Teacher's Journal.* 13:7 (November/December 1979), p. 14. Used by permission.

Birthday Party for Jesus

One of the best ways for young children to understand what it is that we celebrate on Christmas is to have a birthday party for Jesus.

Parents can be asked to provide cupcakes and juice for the party. The classroom can be decorated that day with balloons or streamers. If the children are bringing gifts for the needy or exchanging gifts, they can be brought that day.

Talk with the children about birthdays and celebrations. Explain to them that we have celebrations to share our happiness. Help them to understand that Christmas is Jesus' birthday and that is the reason for the Christmas trees, wreaths, gift-giving, Christmas lights, Christmas cards, and all the other ways we celebrate the coming of Jesus.

Have Christmas music playing as they enter the room. Before they eat their cupcakes, they should sing a rousing chorus of "Happy Birthday, Jesus" to the familiar melody. This helps them understand the meaning of Christmas. An important part of the party is the reading of the Christmas story from Luke. Gather the children in a circle on the floor and read the story of the very first Christmas. This can be followed by the singing of Christmas carols in which all the children participate.

Roleplaying the Christmas Story

The children will learn more about the Christmas story and remember it longer if they roleplay it. The story of the first Christmas (Luke 2:1-20) can be read from a children's Bible. This can be done by the teacher or by an older child.

The children should be assigned the parts of Mary, Joseph, the innkeeper, the angel, and the shepherds. They can act out the journey to Bethlehem, the innkeeper telling them that there was no room for them at the inn, the angel telling the shepherds the good news that the Savior was born, the shepherds coming to visit Jesus and going back to their flocks. A doll wrapped in a blanket can represent Jesus.

The children will probably want to act out the story several times so that they have the opportunity to play several different characters.

Activities that involve the children such as this one help them to understand the spirit of joy and hope and love that is the Christmas season.

Epiphany

The feast of Epiphany provides the opportunity for us to stop and re-examine the message of the Christmas season. Now that the hustle and bustle of Christmas preparations are past, we must think of Christmas as only the beginning of our search for Jesus. We must continue to look for Him in our lives as the three wise men searched for Him in theirs.

Read or tell the children the marvelous story of the search of the three wise men for the infant Jesus (Matthew 2:1-12). The wise men followed a bright star until they came to where He was. This is an interesting story that can be acted out by the children.

The three kings brought Jesus gifts of gold, frankincense, and myrrh. Help the children to think of gifts that they can offer to Jesus. Gifts of ourselves are the most precious gifts of all. We can offer Him gifts such as prayer and kindness towards others. Encourage the children to draw a picture of the three wise men finding Jesus after their long search.

The story of the three kings is important because it shows that Jesus came for all people. The kings were Gentiles, not Jews, who came from faraway lands. Jesus is for all people everywhere.

chapter 11

Sharing Love
on Valentine's Day

Valentine's Day offers us a time to help the children learn about God's love, the love of their parents and friends, and how they can share that love with others. Children like Valentine's Day and the excitement that surrounds the holiday. Valentine's Day enables us to put love and kindness within the realm of their understanding through valentine activities.

Valentine's Day allows us to celebrate the love God has for each of us. It gives the children the opportunity to extend love to others in their lives.

Some activities that can help the children learn about love through celebrating Valentine's Day follow.

Valentine Pictures

Ask the children a couple weeks before Valentine's Day to bring in pictures of themselves from home. Young children will need a note so that their parents can help them remember. Then make a display on the bulletin board with each child's picture inside an individual red paper heart. Title the display "God Loves Us All."

When the children walk in the room, they will see the display and feel loved. This is a good way of helping children learn about love without words.

Heart Badges

Greet the children by name as they arrive. Present each of the children with a red construction paper heart on which is printed the words "God loves me." Explain to young children what the badges say.

Double-stick tape on the back of each heart will allow the children to wear their badges proudly to the Valentine's Day celebration and home. Children feel special when they wear these badges.

Greeting

Direct the children to form a circle and hold hands. Extend a valentine greeting to the nearest child. Say "Happy Valentine's Day" and give that child's hand a squeeze. That child should pass on the words and the squeeze to the next child and so on around the circle until it comes back to the teacher. Thus, everyone will have the opportunity to give and receive a little love.

Puzzles

Cut out half as many paper hearts as there are children in the class. Use a jagged cut to divide each heart in half. Give the heart halves to the children. Direct them to look for the child who has the other half of the heart. Children should match their halves together to find their partners for the day. The children should sit by their partners and share supplies. Partners can work together on all activities as special friends.

Love

Explain to the children that Valentine's Day comes each February as a special day when people show that they care for one another. Ask the children to name people who show them love such as parents, grandparents, friends, and teachers. Remind them that God loves each of them very much.

Ask the children to tell ways that these people show their love. Parents show love by tucking them in at night. Grandparents read stories to them. Friends play with them. Teachers plan special activities for them. God shows love through the beauty of the world and the people in it who love and care for us.

Many times children do no realize how much they are loved by many people until they have the opportunity to talk about it with others.

Valentine Cards

Children like to make valentines to give to important people in their lives. Valentine handprint cards are unique because they have each

Figure 11-1. Valentine Card.

child's handprint. This makes them special to the giver and to the recipient. A helping hand is an appropriate Valentine's Day symbol.

First give each child a piece of red construction paper. The children should fold their papers so that the ends meet in the middle. The front of the card can be decorated with a heart-shaped doily cut in half to allow the card to open. After pasting the doily in place, finish decorating with self-stick heart seals (see illustration).

Inside the card they can draw a large heart. Younger children may need help. Then each child can press a white handprint inside the heart. A pie pan can hold the paint. Allow the handprint to dry. A small bucket of sudsy water nearby and a towel make cleanup easy.

Then the children can paste white paper hearts on either side of the handprint. One heart can say "Happy Valentine's Day" and the other can have a verse such as "God gave me hands to use each day to show I love you in a special way." These can be duplicated before classtime. The white hearts should be precut for younger children. Children should sign their names to their cards.

These cards are special and the children are proud to take home a card that only they can make. This idea previously appeared in my article "Celebrating God's Love on St. Valentine's Day" in *Catechist* magazine.[1]

Special Delivery Letter

This is a good project to carry out the meaning of Valentine's Day. Encourage the children to write a letter to someone. They can make their own stationery by drawing a large heart on a piece of paper. Inside the heart they can use a ruler to draw horizontal lines on which to write their message. The teacher can also have valentine stationery duplicated for each child before class.

Explain to the children that the message they write can be short. It is the meaning behind it that is important. Be sure they remember to sign their names.

Discuss with the children to whom they might give their letters. Suggestions could be a special relative, an ill classmate, a neighbor who lives alone or a friend. The letters should be delivered by the children in person. This project helps the children understand that it is important to give of oneself.

Heart Shapes

The children can use their creativity on this art project. Let them cut out hearts of various sizes from red construction paper. Hearts can be precut for young children. Give the children a sheet of manilla construction paper.

Encourage the children to use their imaginations to make pictures using various combinations of hearts. Hearts can be made into flowers, animals, or people—wherever their minds take them. When they decide on a picture they like, they can glue the red hearts to the manilla construction paper.

This is a good art activity for children because there is not just one way to do it. The picture can be anything a child wants it to be. Projects such as this that require creativity help the children to become aware of their abilities.

[1] This idea originally appeared in *Catechist* (February 1984), p. 42, and is used here by permission of the publisher, Peter Li, Inc., 2451 East River Road, Dayton, Ohio 45439.

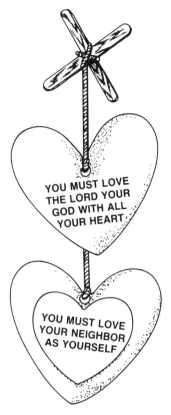

Figure 11-2. Heart Mobile.

Heart Mobile

The children can make heart mobiles to decorate their rooms for Valentine's Day. They add a holiday touch. Then the children can take them home as reminders of the lesson.

The children should cut out two hearts from white paper. Then they should cut out two larger red hearts. The white hearts are glued onto the red hearts.

On one white heart the children print "You must love the Lord your God with all your heart . . . ." On the back print "Matthew 22:37." On the other white heart they should print "You must love your neighbor as yourself." On the back print "Matthew 22:39."

As they do this, the teachers can talk to the children about the message of love that Jesus brought to us. Explain to them that these statements are a summary of everything that He taught.

To make a mobile each child should cross two popsickle sticks and tie them together at right angles with red yarn. Then punch a hole in the top of each heart and thread yarn through the hole. Tie one end of the yarn to the middle of the crossed popsickle sticks and the other end to the first heart. Then extend the yarn to the second heart, which should hang lower than the first (see illustration). These mobiles can be hung from the ceiling with a length of yarn.

These mobiles make a brightly decorated classroom. The Bible verses tie the heart symbol to the love of God and neighbor. In this way we relate God's love and Valentine's Day.

Party Time

Children like to celebrate. A class party for Valentine's Day can be fun. Parents can be asked to provide heart-shaped cookies, juice, cups, and napkins for the party. A few pieces of valentine candy can be tied with a bow in red netting as a favor for each child to take home.

If the children will be exchanging valentines, be sure that each child brings or makes a valentine for every other child. No one should be left out. Decorated shoeboxes or lunch bags can be used for the children to carry home their valentines.

Face Painting

This is a fun party activity. Children enjoy face painting. It's something different and it makes them feel special.

Face paint can be made from powdered tempra paint mixed with face cream. This provides a smooth mixture that is easy to apply with a brush. It will not harm a child's skin and it washes off easily. Red and white face paint can be made up in disposable margarine containers that can be discarded after use.

Paint a heart on each child's cheek. Provide mirrors so that the children can admire how they look.

Valentine Placemats

Valentine placemats are fun to make. They can be used for a class party or taken home to use and are practical as well as decorative.

Show the children how to fringe the edges of sheets of construction paper to make placemats. Half-inch cuts can be made all around red sheets of paper.

Figure 11-3. Valentine Placemat.

The children should cut out six hearts from other colors of paper such as pink, blue, and yellow. These hearts can be precut for younger children. Then the children can glue an arrangement of hearts on their placemats (see illustration). The placemats can be covered with clear self-adhesive covering if desired.

Valentine Search

If the children are not exchanging valentines, they can have a valentine search. Before class begins hide red paper hearts around the classroom for the children to find.

Each of the valentines can bear a Bible verse about love. Bible verses such as the following can be used:

Love is always patient and kind . . .	(1 Corinthians 13:4)
As the Father has loved me, so I have loved you . . .	(John 15:9)
Jesus said, "You must love the Lord your God with all your heart . . ."	(Matthew 22:37)
Love does not come to an end . . .	(1 Corinthians 13:8)
What I command you is to love one another.	(John 15:17)
Let everything you do be done in love . . .	(1 Corinthians 16:14)

Let the children search for the valentines until each child has found three. Read the messages for young children. The children should take home the valentines they find. That way the learning experience of Valentine's Day can be continued at home. Hopefully, the spirit of love that Valentine's Day brings will spread throughout the year.

chapter 12

Rejoicing in the New Life of the Easter Season

Easter is a day of triumph and rebirth. We celebrate Easter in the springtime when we can see signs of new life all around us. This new life reflects the glory of the resurrection and the new life that Jesus brought to us.

We are an Easter people. As Christians, we are filled with joy and hope because Jesus rose on the first Easter Sunday. Every Sunday we rejoice anew in the miracle of the resurrection. Our salvation has been accomplished and heaven awaits us.

The time before Easter is an important time of preparation for the greatest feast of the church year. The word "Lent" means spring. Lent is a time for renewal. Each Lent we need to commit ourselves again to follow Jesus. We need to again make the conscious choice to be a Christian in thought, word, and deed.

Following are some ideas to help children learn about the joy of the Easter season.

Growth

The time of Lent can be explained to the children as a time of change and growth. We must present Lent to the children in terms of their experience. Only in this way will they begin to understand the meaning of this season.

We can explain to the children that just as they change and grow on the outside, so during Lent they need to change and grow on the inside. Let the children name things that they can do now that they couldn't do when they were babies. They can name accomplishments like walking, talking, riding a bike, reading a book.

Then go on to explain that during the time of Lent we need to learn more about God so that we can love Him more. Growing in the love of God is an important part of Lent. Lent is a time to think about God in our minds and hearts. It is a time to tell God more often that we love Him. It is a time to help others as Jesus taught us.

Hopefully, the growing experience and the changes that come about during Lent will become part of the lives of the children after Lent is over. In this way each Lent becomes a stepping stone built upon the growth and changes of the previous Lenten season.

Calling of the Apostles

The story of Jesus calling His first Apostles to follow Him (Matthew 4:18-22) is a good story for the children for the beginning of Lent. Jesus called Peter, Andrew, James, and John to be "fishers of men."

We must explain to the children how we are all followers of Jesus. It is not just the twelve Apostles who were called to do as Jesus said. He calls us now, today, to follow Him in our own way.

People often say that if only they had lived in the time of Jesus, they would have followed Him no matter what happened. We do live in the time of Jesus. He is here present among us. He said to His Apostles after His resurrection "And know that I am with you always, yes to the end of time" (Matthew 28:20). We are to live the life of love that He taught us.

Lent Project

A class Lent project in which all the children can participate helps them live the spirit of Lent. They can grow and change during Lent only if they have the opportunity to put their good intentions into action.

One Lent project could be doing something for someone else each week. Discuss with the children ways in which they can follow Jesus' command that we love one another. Such ways might include helping someone with chores, showing a younger child how to do something, spending time with someone who is lonely, or even extending a simple courtesy such as saying thank you.

Each week the children who do a good deed for someone else could place a leaf on the class giving tree. Such a tree can be cut out of self-adhesive paper in a wood grain pattern. Cut out a trunk and branches and place it on a piece of posterboard. The tree can be displayed in the classroom along with a supply of paper leaves and double-stick tape. This is a good activity for before class as the children are arriving. This way the children who are not adding leaves that week will not be embarrassed in front of the entire class.

The children can discuss in class new ideas for doing God's will. They might want to talk about how it is difficult to be kind and helpful to some people. We can point out to the children how the giving tree is blooming with leaves as the weeks pass. This can be a growing experience for the children.

Lent Chains

The children will like to make Lent chains to help them count the days until Easter. Purple is a traditional color for Lent. Strips of purple paper can be taped together to form the interlocking links of the chain. Tape works better than glue at keeping the links together. The last loop on each chain should be white to signify Easter. One-inch wide strips can be precut for younger children to assemble.

The children can make a 40 link chain with one link for each day of Lent (excluding Sundays) or they can make a seven link chain with one link for each week of Lent. Each day at home the children remove a link from their chains. The number of links remaining shows how many days until Easter. When the white link is taken off, it is Easter at last.

It is a good idea to keep one of the chains hung up in the classroom where the children can see it and remember to keep their chains current. This is a good activity to help children see Lent as the time of preparation for Easter. It can be very useful for children who are too young to read a conventional calendar.

Sweet Potato

Plant a sweet potato in the classroom as a sign of the new life that Jesus brings at Easter. Start the potato on Ash Wednesday or the first time the class meets during Lent. As the plant grows, talk to the class about Easter as a time of hope and new life because of Jesus. The sweet potato will be a reminder to the children all throughout the Lenten season.

To start the sweet potato, cut about two inches off of one end. Stick three toothpicks into the potato to support it on the rim of a glass jar. Fill the jar with water and keep the cut end submerged.

Water should be added every couple of days. Keep the plant in a sunny window. Soon roots will appear followed by tiny shoots. Green leaves soon follow. Some potatoes do sprout more quickly than others. When the sweet potato has become a green, leafy plant, transfer it to a flower pot. Sit the cut end on the bottom, without toothpicks. It will continue to grow in water for weeks. This idea was previously published in my article "12 Activities for Lent" in *Religion Teacher's Journal.*[1]

Signs of New Life

Discuss with the children the signs of new life in the spring that they can see all around them. Young children should learn to view Easter as a time of new life. The theology of the resurrection is beyond their comprehension. Signs of new life are within the realm of their experience and understanding. Talk about:

> Budding trees
> Blooming flowers
> Plants growing
> Green grass
> Baby birds
> Baby animals
> Butterflies

Have on hand an assortment of springtime objects such as a tree branch with buds, pussy willows, and daffodils that the children can touch and examine. The children learn so much more when they can see and touch things as well as hear about them.

Let the children tell about the signs of spring that they have seen. Encourage them to bring in signs of spring from their own yards to share with the class. The children will need parental guidance since some plants are poisonous. This activity will help the children to associate the signs of new life all around them with the new life of Easter. With the children participating in the activity, it becomes a real learning experience for all of them.

Butterfly Symbol

The butterfly is an excellent symbol of resurrection. It can help us understand the meaning not only of Jesus' resurrection, but our resur-

[1]Previously published in *Religion Teacher's Journal* (February 1983), pp. 6-7, published by Twenty-Third Publications, P.O. Box 180, Mystic, CT 06355. Used by permission.

rection when we go to heaven. Young children can come to associate the beautiful butterfly with Easter.

Explain to the children the fascinating story of how a fuzzy caterpillar spins a cocoon around itself. They may have seen a cocoon suspended from a leaf or twig. Inside the cocoon the caterpillar gradually changes into a butterfly. First it sheds its skin and then wings form. When spring comes, the butterfly emerges from the cocoon and flies away.

Try to find pictures of the various stages of metamorphasis in children's nature magazines. It is so much easier to explain to the children with the aid of pictures. Also it is easier for them to understand if they can see the process.

Tell the children that the beautiful butterfly reminds us of the new life that Jesus brings to us at Easter. Encourage them to look for butterflies when they are outside.

Tissue Butterflies

The children can make their own colorful butterflies to take home as symbols of the Easter season.

Lovely butterflies can be made from the multicolored tissue paper sold in variety stores for wrapping gifts. It usually combines various hues of two complimentary colors. Each child should cut out three identical pieces in a butterfly shape. Provide a cardboard pattern of a butterfly for the children to use. Pieces can be precut for younger children.

The children assemble their pieces of tissue together using spring-type clothespins for the bodies of the butterflies. Gather the tissue shapes together in the middle and secure with a clothespin. Gently pull apart the tissue wings.

Add a colorful pipe cleaner for the antennae. Hook it onto the butterfly with the clothespin. Then curve the two ends of the pipe cleaner to look like antennae. This adds a finishing touch to the butterfly (see illustration).

New Life Collage

The children can make a collage of new life pictures to help them learn and remember signs of the Easter season. Pictures of flowers, trees, birds, and butterflies are some that can be used for this project. Garden catalogs are often good sources for pictures of flowers and plants.

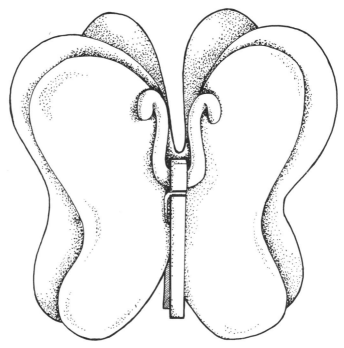

Figure 12-1. Tissue Butterfly.

All pictures should be precut for the children. Otherwise the search through magazines and the process of cutting out the pictures can take up the entire class period. The children should be allowed to select whichever pictures are the most meaningful to them. Children can glue the pictures onto a piece of construction paper. The pictures are glued in a random manner with one picture overlapping another picture to make a collage.

The collages should be labeled "New Life at Easter" or something similar. This will help the children remember and aid their parents in reinforcing the learning at home.

Craft activities aid comprehension and understanding. They encourage learning and make it fun. As with all activities, variety is important. The collage is adaptable to many lessons, but it becomes boring if done lesson after lesson.

A new life collage carries out the theme of the new life Jesus brings at Easter. It helps the children visualize the concepts that they are learning. The bright, colorful collage is a visual interpretation of the hope of the Easter season. It is a good learning activity because it puts an abstract concept into concrete terms.

Egg Carton Flowers

One sign of new life in spring is the profusion of flowers blooming in the warm sun. Children can create their own flowers from egg cartons. They cut apart the individual egg sections from blue, yellow, and pink egg cartons to make lovely pastel flowers.

A pipe cleaner of a coordinating color is pushed through the bottom of each egg section to form a stem. Two green leaves should be cut from green construction paper for each stem. The leaves should remain attached to each other by a band of paper. A pipe cleaner can be pushed through the middle band to attach the leaves to the stem.

The children can use three flowers, one of each color, for a flower arrangement. Use a styrofoam cup for a vase. Turn the cup upside down and push the three stems through the bottom of the cup. Vary the heights to make the arrangement interesting (see illustration).

Glue a colorful strip of paper around the cup for a border. This adds a finishing touch. The flower arrangement is sturdy enough to be placed almost anywhere. Assembling it is easy enough that even a very young child can do it and be pleased with the results.

Figure 12-2. Egg Carton Flowers.

Easter Cards

Encourage the children to share the joy of the Easter season with their families and friends. Provide a variety of materials so that the children can create Easter greeting cards for the important people in their lives.

New life symbols such as flowers, bunnies, or butterflies are appropriate for Easter cards. An angel announcing the news of the resurrection is also a meaningful symbol of Easter. A fun and attractive way to make greeting cards is to let the children cut the shapes of their choosing from wallpaper sample books. The bright, colorful shapes can then be glued onto the front of construction paper cards.

Inside the card can be an Easter greeting and the child's name. The children will enjoy the process of creating and the sense of accomplishment that goes with it. The recipients of the cards will be pleased to received a card obviously made with love.

Easter Story

We are a people of hope because of the first Easter. We can share the message of the first Easter by reading the story of what took place to the children from a children's Bible.

Encourage the children to consider the meaning of the story. Ask them questions to help them think. Ask how the two women felt when they saw that the tomb was empty. Ask about what the Apostles thought when they first saw the risen Jesus. Explain to older children that it was not until after the resurrection that Jesus' followers really understood that He was the Messiah.

Let the children role play the Easter story. This will help them learn and understand this story. For role playing the Easter story can be divided into three parts.

The first story is Matthew 28:1-10 or Mark 16:1-10. This is the account of the discovery of the empty tomb by Mary Magdala and another Mary, the angel's message that Jesus is risen, and His appearance to the two women. Players needed to act out this story are Mary Magdala, Mary, the angel, and Jesus.

The second story can be based on Luke 24:13-33. It tells of Jesus' appearance to two of His disciples on the road to Emmaus. The characters needed are Cleopas, another disciple, and Jesus.

The third part of the Easter story is based on John 20:19-29. It tells of how Jesus appeared to His Apostles. Thomas, who was not there at the time, did not believe. Then Jesus appeared to him also. The characters needed are various Apostles, Thomas, and Jesus.

Different children can participate in the different stories so that all of the children in the class can have a part to play. As the narrative is read by the teacher, the children can act out their roles.

New Life Tree

An attractive and meaningful classroom decoration is a new life tree. A bare tree branch about three to four feet tall is placed in a container of dirt. The children decorate it with paper cutouts of signs of new life of the Easter season.

Each child can choose an appropriate symbol to make and cut out of colorful construction paper. Colors such as blue, red, yellow, green,

Figure 12-3. New Life Tree.

and orange work well. Symbols can be precut for younger children. Each child should have a different symbol. Each symbol should have a hole punched in the top and yarn threaded through to make a hangar.

Then the children can hang their new life symbols on the tree (see illustration). This will remind them that Jesus brought new life at Easter. Some of the symbols that can be used are:

Leaf

Duckling

Bird

Butterfly

Lamb

Egg

Child

Sun

Chick

Frog

Flower

Squirrel

Bunny

The tree decoration can also be used throughout the year as a seasonal or holiday decoration. It can be decorated with leaves, hearts, or flowers.

Easter Customs

Encourage the children to share their families' Easter customs with the class. It makes the children feel proud to have something to contribute to the class. The sharing of ideas can be a source of learning for all the children.

Ask the children questions to help them remember such as:

Will you have grandparents visiting for Easter?
Are you having a special Easter dinner?
Will you be going to any of the special church services?
Do you usually get an Easter basket with eggs and candy?
Are you going to an Easter egg hunt?
Does your family do something special on Easter?

Explain to the children that we do all these things because we are rejoicing in the new life that Jesus has given us. We surround ourselves with signs of new life such as lilies and Easter eggs as symbols of the meaning of Easter.

Paper Eggs

Let the children decorate the classroom for Easter. The Easter egg has long been a sign of new life associated with the Easter season.

Provide large paper egg shapes cut out of manilla construction paper for the children to decorate. Provide a variety of colors of markers and encourage the children to draw on their eggs. Young children can make stripes and zigzag lines across their eggs. Older children might wish to draw swirly designs and flowers or bunnies on theirs.

The egg decorations should be done entirely by the children with their own ideas. Be sure that the children put their names on the back of their eggs. Then they can punch a hole in the top and thread a length of yarn through it. This way the eggs can be hung from the ceiling to provide a festive classroom. The children will feel proud to see their artwork displayed. This project will also help them to see Easter as a time of joy.

Paper Flowers

Children enjoy making a garden of springtime flowers. Flowers are a sign of new life as they bloom at Easter time.

Each child can make a construction paper flower in any shape desired. A round circle of a contrasting color paper can be used for the center of the flower. Each flower should be taped to the end of a straw. Then green leaves can be cut out and taped about halfway down the straw. So that each flower will stand up by itself, plant each in a small paper cup of sand. If desired, cover the cup with construction paper (see illustration).

All the spring flowers can be grouped together on a windowsill or shelf for a springtime garden in the classroom. The flowers will make a bright grouping. Each flower can be as unique as the individual child. Together they make a wonderful display.

Craft projects such as this help children to remember that Easter is a time of new life. They will retain the message of the lesson longer. Be sure to praise the children for their originality and creativity. Quietly help

147

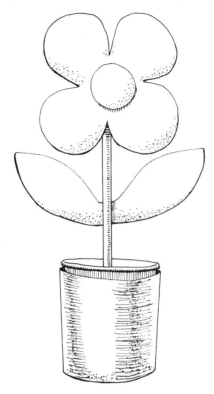

Figure 12-4. Paper Flower.

those children who have difficulty with scissors. Always remember that it is the learning that takes place that is important. Art and craft projects generate joy in children and Easter is the season of joy.

Children should take their flowers home at the last class before Easter vacation to bloom at home.

Coloring Eggs

A fun activity that has traditionally been part of Easter preparations is the coloring of Easter eggs. Children can understand that eggs are a sign of new life. Chicks, ducklings, and even baby birds hatch from eggs.

Inexpensive egg coloring can be made from food coloring. To each one half cup of boiling water add one teaspoon vinegar. Then add about 20 drops of food coloring to each cup and mix with a spoon.

If the children want to do so, they can write their names or make a design on the hardboiled eggs before they are colored with a white crayon. The wax will not take the dye and the name or design will remain white after the egg is colored.

The children dip an egg in each cup of dye until the desired shade is reached. Then they pull out the egg with a spoon. An egg carton can be used for a drying rack. Salad oil rubbed on each finished egg with a paper towel will give the egg a shine.

Easter Baskets

Children like to make Easter baskets. These can be used as favors for the "Meals on Wheels" program or a similar service. These organizations deliver hot meals once a day to those who are unable to do their own cooking. Check with the person in charge for a day and plan to deliver the baskets to the volunteers who deliver the meals.

Easter baskets can be made from the green pint baskets that strawberries come in from the grocery store. The children can weave thin strips of ribbon through the openings in the baskets. Green Easter grass can be used to fill the baskets. On top of the grass the children can put Easter candy. A large pipe cleaner can be hooked onto either side for a handle. This method makes festive and decorative baskets that can be used as storage containers after Easter is over.

Another way for children to make Easter baskets is using clean, empty half-pint milk cartons. Cut off the top part of the carton. Then the children can cover the outside of the carton with construction paper. On the front of each carton they can glue an Eater bunny cutout that is twice as high as the carton. Then they can fill the basket with Easter grass and candy. These make nice individual Easter baskets and are very inexpensive to make.

Easter Party

Since Easter is a feast of great joy, it can be celebrated with a party in the classroom. This helps the children to view Easter as a time of happiness. Children love parties.

Notes can go home the week before requesting parent help in providing treats for the children's celebration. Hopefully, the children can help their parents prepare the food at home.

Popular treats are Easter basket cupcakes. Color the frosting green with food coloring. Tint shredded coconut green also. The coconut should be put on the frosting to look like grass. Put four jelly beans in the middle for Easter eggs. As a decorative touch a curved pipe cleaner can be pushed into the cupcake to look like a handle. The handle cannot be used to actually carry the cupcake.

Another party treat is to use the popular rice cereal and marshmallow mixture. Spread mixture in a thin layer in a pan. Cut out shapes with a buttered bunny cookie cutter. Use decorator icing to outline each bunny close to the outside edge. Then add an eye with a drop of frosting and a miniature marshmallow to each bunny for a fluffy tail.

Egg Hunt

A traditional part of the Easter celebration is the Easter egg hunt. Children enjoy searching for plastic Easter eggs hidden around the classroom. It is best to limit the number of eggs that can be found by each child so all the children will have the opportunity to find some eggs.

The egg hunt can be a fun learning activity if a Bible verse from the Easter story is hidden inside of each egg. As the children find an egg, they can read the Bible verse.

Bible verses that reflect the joy and hope of Easter should be used. Some suitable verses include the following:

> He is not here; he has risen . . . (Luke 24:6)
> . . . Proclaim the Good News to all creation. (Mark 16:16)
> . . . Peace be with you. (Luke 24:36)
> . . . Happy are those who have not seen and yet believe. (John 20:29)
> . . . And know that I am with you always; yes, to the end of time. (Matthew 28:20)

The children should take home the eggs and Bible verses that they find as reminders of the joy and hope that Easter brings to us as Christians.

chapter 13

Concluding Remarks

Above all religious education seeks to help children build a relationship with God. In his book *First Things,* Rod Brownfield states what religion is:

> Religion is so many things and so varied that encyclopedists are reluctant to set down a hard definition. But *re-ligio,* in its Latin root, seems to have meant to tie, to fasten, to bind. If we can accept this root meaning, we still have to ask: What is it that religion is supposed to bind? And the answer is: Just about everything—man to God, God to man, man to his fellowmen, man to space and to time, and to the universe, to eternity, to all of life.[1]

Christianity is a way of life to be lived. We need to help children learn about God's love for His people and how He wants us to love Him and to love others.

We can begin by helping the children to see that they are special, wonderful individuals created by God. We must help them to discover that God loves each of them just as they are. Then they will be able to accept God's love for them and to reach out to Him in return.

We can help the children discover God's presence in their lives through the world and the people around them. The more the children learn about God and come to know Him through His creation, the more they will love Him. Creation puts the experience of God's love on a personal level for the children.

Concepts and ideas that are presented to children must be related to their own lives. Only in this way can true learning take place. As Jesus

[1]Rod Brownfield, *First Things: A Handbook for Beginners in Religious Education* (Dayton, Ohio: Pflaum Press, 1973), p. 11. Used by permission of Pflaum Press.

taught His followers through parables, so we must teach children through the experiences in their lives.

Children learn by doing. Lessons must be presented in a variety of ways that actively involve the children in the learning process. Children remember more of what they do. All activities must reflect and reinforce the message of the lesson. This aids understanding and retention of the material being presented. We must help the children discover how the information applies to their own lives. We must also help them learn from the ideas and experiences of others.

We need to encourage the children to help others as Jesus taught us. The children need to learn that Jesus brought a message of love for all people. As members of God's family, it is our responsibility to care about all people.

We can help children come to know God through Bible stories of His love for His people. The life and teachings of Jesus can provide a model for them of how they are to love God and others always.

We must help the children to seek God's help in all that they do through prayer. In this we must set an example. Prayer must be an important part of our lives. We must always remember for Whom it is that we do this. As teachers we must ask God's help in our role as mediators of His message.

We can help the children learn about God and His love through things that are important in their lives. Holidays offer us the opportunity to celebrate together the love that God has for each of us.

We must help the children seek God in all that they do. We must equip them with the desire and the skills necessary to continue to seek God's presence in their lives. Religious education of children is the beginning of the quest for a relationship with God. It is part of the life-long search to love God and to do His will.

Bibliography

BOOKS

Borba, Michele and Craig, *Self-Esteem: A Classroom Affair.* Minneapolis, MN: Winston Press, 1978.

Bowman Jr., Locke E., *Teacher Improvement: Practice, Study.* Scottsdale, AZ: National Teacher Education Program, 1976.

Brownfield, Rod, *First Things: A Handbook for Beginners in Religious Education.* Dayton, OH: Pflaum Press, 1973.

Canfield, Jack, and Harold C. Wells, *100 Ways to Enhance Self-Concept in the Classroom.* Englewood Cliffs, NJ: Prentice-Hall, Inc., 1976.

Chernoff, Goldie Taub, *Puppet Party.* New York: Scholastic, Inc., 1971.

Cooke, S.S.J., Sister Anne, *Lifelines for Religion Teachers.* Mystic, CT: Twenty-Third Publications, 1977.

Dale, Sharon, *God's People Together in Christ* Vacation Bible School Series Planning Guide. Minneapolis, MN: Augsburg Publishing House, 1980.

Foley, Rita, *Create! The Art of Teaching Religion.* New York: William H. Sadlier, Inc., 1982.

Gordon, Thomas, *TET: Teacher Effectiveness Training,* New York: David McKay Co., Inc., 1974.

Landry, Rev. Carey, and Carol Jean Kinghorn, *Celebrating Jesus.* Phoenix, AZ: North American Liturgy Resources, 1977.

Mackenzie, Joy, *The Big Book of Bible Crafts and Projects.* Nashville, TN: Impact Books, 1981.

Mueller, Jeanne Coolahan, *Living in God's Love* Vacation Bible School Planning Guide. Minneapolis, MN: Augsburg Publishing House, 1981.

Rezy, Carol, *Liturgies for Little Ones.* Notre Dame, IN: Ave Marie Press, 1978.

Skinner, Donna, *File Folder Learning Centers for Bible Study Fun.* Cincinnati, OH: The Standard Publishing Co., 1982.

TIMMERMAN, M.H.S.H., MARGARET, *How To Be A Very, Very, Very, Very Good Catechist.* Mystic, CT: Twenty-Third Publications, 1981.

PERIODICALS

CLARK, CAROL, "Arrangement of the Creche," *Religion Teacher's Journal,* November/December 1979.

JANAS, GINNY, "Summer Celebrations," *Religion Teacher's Journal,* May/June 1980.

KIRK, PATRICK, "Questions: Directions for Growth," *Catechist,* February 1981.

LILJA, JOAN, "Echo Pantomimes Intrigue Teachers and Learners," *Church Teachers Magazine,* March/April/May 1983.

McGUIRK, DONN P., "Board Games For Review Can Be Made Easily From Everyday File Folders," *Church Teachers Magazine,* January/February 1983.

MATHSON, PATRICIA L., "Advent Family Day," *Today's Parish,* October 1983.

———, "Building Community in the Classroom," *Religion Teacher's Journal,* October 1984.

———, "12 Activities for Lent," *Religion Teacher's Journal,* February 1983.

———, "Vacation Bible School," *Catechist,* February 1983.

———, "Celebrating God's Love on St. Valentine's Day," *Catechist,* February 1984.

Index

Fishing for Bible verses, 79-80
Flannelboard stories, 83
Flowers:
    candy cup, 37
    paper, 147-48
Food collection, 107-08
Forgiveness, 49
Formal prayer, 66
Friendly actions, 48
Friendship chains, 22-23

G

Games:
    charades, 42
    cover-up, 95-96
    get acquainted, 20
    guessing, 39
    helpers, 53
    life of Jesus, 93-94
    reviewing with, 89-103
Genesis, 31, 74
Gestures, 66-67, 70
Get acquainted games, 20
Gift certificates, 121-22
Gifts, God's, 31
Goals:
    activities to reinforce, 3
    formulating, 2-3
    selection of, 2-3
    setting, 2-3
    word list to describe, 203
God:
    image of, 7
    letters to, 63-64
God's People Together in Christ (Dale),
    69
Good Samaritan, 53-54
Gordon, Thomas, 7-8
Gospels, 74
Growth, 137-38
Guessing game, 39

H

Hand turkeys, 106
Happy day cards, 52-53
Hearing 45

Heart:
    badges, 129-30
    mobile 133-34
    shapes 132
Hello game, 20
Helpers, 11
    game, 53
Helping hands, 54-55
How to Be a Very, Very, Very, Very
        Good Catechist (Timmerman),
        2, 50, 54

I

"I Am Special" badges, 9-10
Ideas, abstract, 3
Instruments, 70
Interviews, recorded, 23
Introductions, 20-21
Isaiah, 116

J

Janas, Ginny, 71
Jesse tree, 116-18
Jesus, using examples in teaching, 3
John, 113-44, 150

K

Kinghorn, Carol Jean, 61
Kirk, Patrick, 26
Knowledge, questions to test, 26

L

Landry, Carey, 61
Learning, 1-2, 19, 56
    activities related to goals, 2
    centers, 89
    small groups, 27
    through senses, 44-45
    to care, 47
    question types, 26
Lent, 137
    chains, 139
Letters, 21
    to God, 63-64

Puzzles, 77-78, 82, 130
Puppet Party (Chernoff), 44
Puppets, 43-44

Q

Questionnaires, 21
Questions:
  levels of, 26
  to build faith, 27
  to guide discussion, 53
Quotes, Bible, 96-97

R

Religion, 151
Religious development, 5
Religious education, 1
  as ongoing process, 5
  books in, 50
  goal of, 151-52
  importance of questions in, 26
  self-concept, 7
  teaching caring, 47-60
  use of games in, 101
Religious growth, 5
Religious teaching, result of, 47
Research project, 27
Respect, 8
Resurrection, 138, 140
Rezy, Carol, 110
Rhyme puzzles, 77-78
Role models, 47, 60
Role playing, 57-58, 126
Round robin, 78

S

Saints, 27, 59-60
  Francis, 59-60
  Nicholas, 116
Samaritan, 53-54
Seasons, 41-43
Secret friend, 116
Seeds, planting, 36
Self-concept, 14, 17
  in children, 7

Self-esteem:
  activities to develop, 8-17
  effect on children, 7
  sense of self-concept, 7
Self-Esteem: A Classroom Affair
  (Borba), 11, 48
Self-study flash cards, 90
Self-worth, activity for, 11
Senses, 44-45
Service projects, 56-57
Sharing, 19
  activity for, 13
  through discussion, 25-27
Sight, 45
Signs, of new life, 140
Skinner, Donna, 96
Slides, 65
Small groups, in learning, 27
Smell, 45
Smile badges, 48-49
Snowflakes, 120
Songs, with gestures, 71-72
Sorting game, 97-98
Speakers, 58-59
Special delivery letter, 132
Special student activity, 14
Sponge painting, 82-83
Spring, 25, 142
Stories, 50
  flannelboard, 83
  telling, 75
Summer, 42
Sun catchers, 39-40
Sweet potato, 139-40
Symbols, 27

T

Talking, 62
Tape recording, 23
Taste, sense of, 45
Teachers, 8-9
  attitude toward questions, 26
  building community, 19
  language of acceptance, 17
  role in passing on values, 2
  role in religious education, 1
Teacher Improvement (Bowman), 2-3,
  26
Teaching:
  messages of Bible, 73-74